Theory for Performance Studies

"an invaluable book . . . a wonderfully useful and user-friendly précis of the most salient intellectual influences on the meanings of performance. This is a much-needed and important addition to the field."

Gabrielle H. Cody, *Vassar College, New York*

Theory for Performance Studies: A Student's Guide is a clear and concise handbook to the key connections between performance studies and critical theory since the 1960s. Philip Auslander looks at the way the concept of performance has been engaged across a number of disciplines.

Beginning with four foundational figures – Freud, Marx, Nietzsche, and Saussure – Auslander goes on to provide guided introductions to the major theoretical thinkers of the past century, from Althusser to Žižek. Each entry offers biographical, theoretical, and bibliographical information along with a discussion of each figure's relevance to theatre and performance studies and suggestions for future research.

Brisk, thoughtful, and engaging, this is an essential first volume for anyone who works in theatre and performance studies today.

Philip Auslander teaches Performance Studies at the Georgia Institute of Technology and the University of Georgia. His research interests include performance theory, performance and technology, and popular music. He is the author of *Liveness: Performance in a Mediatized Culture* (1999) and editor of *Performance: Critical Concepts* (2003).

Theory for Performance Studies

Studies

A student's guide

Philip Auslander

Routledge
Taylor & Francis Group

LONDON AND NEW YORK

First published 2008
by Routledge
2 Park Square, Milton Park, Abingdon, Oxon OX14 4RN

Simultaneously published in the USA and Canada
by Routledge
270 Madison Ave, New York, NY 10016

Routledge is an imprint of the Taylor & Francis Group, an informa business

© 2008 Philip Auslander

Typeset in Sabon by
Book Now Ltd, London
Printed and bound in Great Britain by
The Cromwell Press, Trowbridge, Wiltshire

British Library Cataloguing in Publication Data
A catalogue record for this book is available from the British Library

Library of Congress Cataloging in Publication Data
Auslander, Philip, 1956–
Theory for performance studies: a student's guide/Philip Auslander.
      p. cm.
Includes bibliographical references.
1. Performing arts–Social aspects. 2. Performing arts–Philosophy. I. Title.

PN1590.S6A885 2007
792.02′2–dc22   2007005254

ISBN10: 0–415–97452–6 (hbk)
ISBN10: 0–415–97453–4 (pbk)
ISBN10: 0–203–94483–6 (ebk)

ISBN13: 978–0–415–97452–3 (hbk)
ISBN13: 978–0–415–97453–0 (pbk)
ISBN13: 978–0–203–94483–7 (ebk)

Contents

Acknowledgments

I would like to thank Bill Germano for recruiting me, and Talia Rodgers for picking up the ball. I would also like to thank the staffs of the various units of the libraries of the University System of Georgia for making it easy to find stuff, and the other libraries that provided access to material. Many people made valuable suggestions in response to on-line or personal queries and generously supplied me with citations or their writings.

To all the people who remember the heady days of "The New Poetics": Without you, a book such as this would not have been possible. (Or necessary!)

For Deanna, with devotion

Introduction

Theory for performance studies – who needs it?

What is theory and why is it important for performance studies?

Theory, from the Greek *theoria*, which means "a viewing" or "spectacle," offers a way of seeing. A theory is something like a conceptual lens, a pair of spectacles, which you use to frame and focus what you're looking at. It is a tool for discerning, deciphering, and making sense.

In my view, performance studies is a paradigm-driven field, by which I mean that it takes the concept of performance as both its object of inquiry and its primary analytical concept (I will explain further shortly). The central question animating the discipline is: "What is performance?" The more contexts in which we look at the concept of performance and the more cases to which we apply it, the better we will be able to answer that question. Or, perhaps it is more accurate to say that we will come up with more and more useful answers to the question, for performance studies is not about discovering a single theory of performance. Any answer to the basic question constitutes a de facto theory of performance, that is, an idea of performance that is used to make sense of various practices and forms of expression. Every theory frames and focuses our attention on some things while leaving other things outside the frame or out of focus. Thus, performance studies is always in search of new theories that might open up new ways of seeing and interpreting performance. Performance studies *is* theory: it is the myriad conceptual tools used to "see" performance.

The approach I take here to looking at the relationship between performance studies and theory is unique. There are already excellent books that offer an overview of the discipline or of the concept of performance: Richard Schechner's *Introduction to Performance Studies* (Routledge, 2nd edition 2006) and Marvin Carlson's *Performance: A Critical Introduction* (Routledge, 2nd edition 2004), respectively. *Theory for Performance Studies* does not survey exclusively those theorists assumed to be central to performance studies (many are absent, in fact) and it is not a guide to key concepts in the field. Rather, it seeks to discuss the various relationships a list of twenty-nine canonical modern and postmodern thinkers have to performance studies. (By canonical, I mean that the importance of these figures is generally accepted in academic circles and that their influence is not confined to performance studies or any other single discipline. These are theorists whose ideas have had broad but unevenly distributed influence over a variety of fields.) In some cases, the thinkers discussed here are central to performance studies (Judith Butler is an example), while in other cases their relationships are more tangential. This inquiry allows the reader to position performance studies in relation to other fields and disciplines that draw from these same thinkers. It provides a guide to what some figures have contributed to the field and how the thought of some others might inspire new directions.

I wrote this book with three audiences in mind. First, it is for undergraduate students in courses on theory and methodology in performance studies. This book complements existing basic texts by providing concise synopses of the ideas of key figures in intellectual history and their relevance to performance studies. It is also to a certain extent a companion volume to *Performance: Critical Concepts*, which I edited for Routledge (2003). I have cited contributions to that collection here where it was reasonable to do so. The present book provides further intellectual context for the essays collected there.

Second, this book is for graduate students. Not only will it serve masters or doctoral students seeking theoretical frameworks for thesis or dissertation research, but also it will prove useful as they prepare for a career in teaching.

Finally, *Theory for Performance Studies* is intended for teachers and scholars of theatre and performance who need a resource to help them introduce students to contemporary theoretical perspectives and who are themselves interested in how these perspectives might speak more directly to performance studies.

Theory and performance studies: the disciplinary context

In some contexts, I would characterize theatre studies and performance studies as closely related fields that are nevertheless quite different in significant ways. In a nutshell, I believe theatre studies to be an *object-driven* discipline. That is, there is an object (or a set of objects, if you prefer) called theatre, and the purpose of theatre studies is to study that object using a variety of tools (some historical, for example, some critical or analytical). Even while acknowledging that what "theatre" is may vary culturally and along other lines, and while there may be disagreement about whether or not a particular object belongs to the class "theatre," there must be a general agreement that we know what theatre is for the discipline to function (just as there must be some general understanding of what art is in art history, what music is in musicology, etc.).

As I have said, I consider performance studies to be a *paradigm-driven* discipline. There is no object (or set of objects) called performance(s) the study of which performance studies takes as its purpose. Rather, there is an idea, performance, that serves as the paradigmatic starting point for any inquiry that occurs within the disciplinary realm. In principle, this paradigm can function as a lens through which to examine almost anything. The project of performance studies as a discipline is to trace the paradigm through analysis of the myriad contexts in which it appears and to which it can be applied.

The two disciplines have different relationships to theory of the sort under discussion here. Theatre studies is the older discipline and was based largely in a positivistic approach to the history of theatre, until the early 1980s when many scholars began to look at theatre through other theoretical lenses, including many represented by the figures discussed here. From that point on, theatre studies has become a discipline increasingly shaped by theory, as can be seen, for example, by comparing the kinds of scholarly articles published in *Theatre Journal*, which began publication in 1979, with those that appeared in its predecessor, the *Educational Theatre Journal* (1949–78).

Performance studies, by contrast, came into being as a theoretical discipline. Emerging originally as a confluence of ideas drawn from humanistic and social scientific disciplines that included theatre, anthropology (including the study of folklore and oral traditions), and sociology, performance studies sought to focus on the idea of performance, understood to be broader and more inclusive than theatre, through the lenses provided by these and other disciplines. That the field had a theoretical slant is evident in the title of the first book by Richard Schechner, one of its founders: *Essays on Performance Theory: 1970–1976* (originally published 1977; Routledge, 2nd edition 2003). Over time, performance studies, too, has been reshaped through the influence of theory. Arguably, the original confluence of theatre, anthropology, and sociology has yielded first to poststructuralist and feminist theoretical approaches, then to the influence of cultural studies and postcolonial theory.

I offer these definitions and tell this story in part to explain why it is important to look at performance studies from a broad theoretical perspective. As an inherently interdisciplinary discipline, performance studies is open to intellectual influence from all directions – one never knows what set of ideas will open up a new way of understanding performance. The multidisciplinarity, not only of performance studies but also of the growing academic interest in performance, is very clear in the sources of the books and articles cited in the bibliographies included here, whose fields of origin include, besides theatre and performance studies: sociology, anthropology, speech communication, literature, music, philosophy, dance studies, cultural studies, geography, psychology, and political and cultural theory, among many others.

In assembling these bibliographies, I have not made a sharp distinction between theatre studies and performance studies, primarily for practical reasons. When most of the theorists under consideration here discuss performance, theatre is their primary reference point and they implicitly understand performance primarily in terms of theatre and theatricality. To have limited the cited sources only to those that truly focus on performance and performativity, but not theatre, would have been unnecessarily restrictive. The happy result is that the present volume will be of as much value to theoretically inclined students of theatre as it is to those in performance studies. I have tried, however, to focus the bibliographic citations mostly on sources that discuss *performance* rather than literary interpretations of plays, for example. I have included such material only where it seemed particularly apposite.

Conversations

This book is not only a guide to how theory since the 1960s has transformed the intellectual landscape in which performance studies finds its place, but also an invitation to join in the conversation – regardless of the theoretical stands one adopts.

The contemporary theoretical perspectives introduced in this book did not emerge miraculously, *ex nihilo*, from the solitary minds of their authors. They were developed in conversation with those who preceded them. In this regard, four theoretical predecessors are particularly important: Sigmund Freud, Karl Marx, Friedrich Nietzsche, and Ferdinand de Saussure. Together with others, these four constitute a common context for theoretical discourse since the mid-twentieth century. Indeed, their concepts and questions continue to set the agenda for contemporary theory. Whether or not one embraces them, one must have a basic understanding of their contributions. Therefore Part I of this book is devoted to these four predecessors to contemporary theory and also examines their direct contributions to the study of performance.

Just as the theorists introduced in this book were engaged in dialogue with their own theoretical predecessors, I invite today's students of performance to be in conversation with the theories and theorists described here. Whether or not one ultimately declares oneself a Kristevan or Foucauldian or Lacanian – or, for that matter, a Marxist or Freudian or Nietzschean or Saussurean – it is important to attend to the questions these thinkers raise. What happens to our view of performance and the way it produces meaning, for instance, when we question the nature of language? Does language represent a natural correspondence between word and external referent, or, as structuralists would argue, is language a semiotic system in which the linguistic sign is both arbitrary and based on difference?

How to use this book

This book is designed to be useful. I assume that most readers will not read it from cover to cover, but will go to it for help with particular theorists and theories. The four predecessors introduced in Part I are presented in alphabetical order by last name, as are the twenty-five entries in Part II. Every entry in the book has three main sections: a list of key concepts, the main body of the text, and further reading.

At the beginning of each entry is a short bulleted list of key concepts, which I have identified as particularly important for students of performance to understand. These concepts are listed in the order of their appearance in the main text.

The main body of each entry begins with a brief biographical sketch. In the discussion that follows, key concepts are highlighted where they are first explained. Thus a reader interested in one particular key concept can quickly scan the entry for the discussion of it. I also offer some discussion of the theorist's ideas directly related to performance and possible implications of the theory for performance studies. I do not indicate all the possible implications, however, as if that were possible: these discussions are intended to be suggestive, not comprehensive.

Finally, each entry has a further reading section which includes two subsections: first, a "By" subsection listing primary texts; second, an "About" subsection listing texts about the theorist as well as texts on performance that include a significant discussion of the theorist or application of the theorist's ideas. Within each of these subsections, one or two key texts are indicated with asterisks. I recommend these as starting points for further reading.

This book suggests multiple possible ways that we might see performance. Although the theorists I explore here are sometimes difficult to understand on first contact, I believe that they are well worth the effort. My goal has been to provide initial access to their work, to explain their key concepts, and to give suggestion for further study. As readers move beyond my short introductions to the primary and secondary texts listed in the Further Reading sections, I fully expect that they will develop more complex and subtle understandings of the potential contributions of these theorists to the academic study of performance than I can present here. Happy theorizing!

Part I
Predecessors

1   Sigmund Freud

Key concepts

- psychoanalysis
- unconscious
- repression
- Oedipus Complex
- illusion

Sigmund Freud (1856–1939) was born to a Jewish family in Freiburg, Germany. The Freuds moved to Vienna when he was 4. Throughout his school years, he was an outstanding student. He graduated with distinction from the Gymnasium in 1878 and took his medical degree at the University of Vienna in 1881. In 1885 he won a modest medical scholarship that allowed him to travel to Paris where he worked under Jean-Martin Charcot (1825–93) at the Salpêtrière hospital. Freud was fascinated with Charcot's work on hysteria, which he treated as a disease, and his use of hypnotism to reproduce symptoms of hysteria in his patients. In 1886 Freud began his practice as a physician in Vienna, where his focus was likewise on nervous disorders. Vienna remained his home until 1938, when he was forced to flee Austria for England after the Nazi *Anschluss*. He died in London the following year.

Freud was the founder of **psychoanalysis**. In a 1922 essay for a general audience, Freud provided three interrelated definitions of psychoanalysis: (1) a discipline focused on investigating the unconscious, (2) a therapeutic method for treating nervous disorders, and (3) a growing body of research data ("Two Encyclopedia Articles"). Together these three definitions provide a helpful introduction to Freud's work.

First, Freud defines psychoanalysis as an academic discipline whose aim is to investigate and analyze otherwise inaccessible mental processes, which Freud describes as the workings of the **unconscious**. The unconscious is, most simply put, the non-conscious part of the mind. As such it affects conscious thought and behavior but is not directly accessible for interpretation. Freud's innovation in psychology was not the discovery of the unconscious per se (others, including NIETZSCHE, had written about it), but rather the means to access and interpret it. He did so through analysis of slips of the tongue, jokes, and above all dreams, which he called the "royal road" to the unconscious. Dreams, Freud believed, represent fulfillments of unconscious wishes and desires that the conscious mind censors because they are socially taboo or a threat to the integrity of the self. For Freud, the content of the unconscious is essentially those drives which are inadmissible to the conscious self and are therefore forced out of consciousness through mechanisms of **repression**. These include drives and memories related to the "primal scene" (childhood recollection of seeing one's parents having sex) as well as taboo desires related to the Oedipus Complex. Although repressed, they inevitably resurface in dreams, "Freudian slips," and other forms of expression and can become the bases for neuroses if not addressed therapeutically.

The **Oedipus Complex** is particularly important to Freud's understanding of human consciousness and the origin of nervous disorders. The name comes from the Greek legend of Oedipus, who unwittingly kills his father, marries his mother, and then blinds himself when he realizes what he has done. For Freud, the Oedipus Complex concerns the young child's attraction to the parent of the opposite sex and jealousy of the parent of the same sex. Although girls and boys experience this attraction and negotiate this complex differently, in both cases the goal is to transition from jealousy of the same-sex parent to identification with her or him. Freud believes that the Oedipus Complex is a universal event, and that the failure to negotiate it successfully is the primary cause of nervous disorders.

Freud's second definition of psychoanalysis is as a therapeutic method for treating nervous disorders. The method largely involves uncensored, free association by the patient (analysand), who lies on a couch while the analyst sits behind her or him and listens for subtle manifestations to the unconscious processes that are the source of the neurosis. The primary medium of psychoanalysis, then, is the spoken word. Indeed, one of Freud's early patients aptly characterized psychoanalysis as the "talking cure." But it does not take words at face value. Rather it sifts through the language of the conscious mind for traces of the unconscious. The speaking human being is approached as a divided subject, a site of conflict between conscious and unconscious drives that do not come together into a single, integrated, whole self. Freud's third definition of psychoanalysis is as a growing body of active scientific research, including case studies, research data on the mind and brain, and interpretations of other aspects and works of culture. Indeed, Freud did not restrict himself to analyzing individual human subjects, nor did he ignore other fields of academic research in the natural sciences and humanities. In fact, he was a prolific interpreter of culture, approaching it through scholarship in archeology, anthropology, linguistics, and literature.

Freud's view of culture was not particularly optimistic, however. In *The Future of an Illusion* (1927), Freud suggests that belief in God is a neurotic wish fulfillment. If an **illusion** is something that one very much wishes to be true, then belief in God is, for Freud, an illusion. As children we had parents to protect us from reality and, above all, to help us believe that everything will be okay, that we are safe amid the storm. (Of course, the parent knows that such assurances are ultimately illusory.) As adults, we still need that kind of assurance in the illusion of safety and security, but we no longer have our parents to provide it. And that is the function of religion. It is a projection of what we want to be true, of a God who is the ultimate, ideal parent. In this respect, Freud speculates, society's belief in God is something like a collective neurosis arising from the Oedipus Complex. In *The Future of an Illusion*, Freud suggests that as human society continues to evolve, to mature, thereby outgrowing childhood wishes and desires, it will outgrow its need for such a father figure and modern reason will replace illusion. Just a few years later, however, in *Civilization and its Discontents* (1930), he argues that civilization can exist only if human beings repress their instincts, which repression leads inevitably to neurosis and misery that expresses itself in violence. In this later work, the chance that a mature, illusion-free society will come into being seems slim indeed.

Many writers have suggested that psychoanalysis and theatre are closely related to one another and implicated in one another's histories. The first phase of psychoanalysis was inspired by Freud's seeing Charcot's medical theatre demonstrations, in which he would treat hysterical patients with hypnosis; as Elin Diamond has argued, the female patients in these demonstrations were presented in ways that resembled the representation of the hysterical woman on the melodramatic stage ("Realism's Hysteria," p. 14). In a reference to Aristotle's theory of tragedy, Freud referred to his early therapeutic approach as "cathartic," while his later thought revolved around the Oedipus Complex, which derived from the plot of Sophocles's play *Oedipus the King*. Freud also used theatrical terminology to describe key elements of his theory as, for example, in his concept of the "primal scene."

Additionally, many commentators see strong parallels between theatre and the process of psychoanalysis. Freddie Rokem observes:

> Both theatre and psychoanalysis search the individual's private psychic life which becomes public or receives a public form of expression through these two activities. When the private is made public, theatre and psychoanalysis become effective. Or, to put it the other way around: they are both public forms of privacy. . . . [T]hey both seek to overcome [the opposition of public and private] through language. In the patient's speech and the actor's dialogue, the private realm becomes real. . . . [T]hrough this exposure of private fantasies and associations, the patient experiences a kind of purgative or cathartic effect traditionally associated with theatre audiences.
>
> (Rokem, "Acting and Psychoanalysis," p. 179)

The connections between theatre and psychoanalysis have had many manifestations, ranging from the profound influence of Freudian thought on modern drama, to the use of psychoanalytical theory to examine every aspect of theatrical performance, including dramatic texts, acting, theatrical production, stage fright, and theatre architecture (see Sander).

Freud himself enjoyed the theatre and wrote well-known analyses of *Oedipus the King* and Shakespeare's *Hamlet* as literary works in *The Interpretation of Dreams*. In a short essay of 1904, he also expounds his own psychoanalytical theory of dramatic representation, a theory that strongly emphasizes symbolic wish-fulfillment and the spectator's identification with the character: "The sympathetic witnessing of a dramatic performance fulfills the same function for the adult as does play for the child, whose besetting hope of being able to do what the adult does it gratifies" ("Psychopathic Characters," p. 144). (For Freud, it seems, the theatre, like religion, gratifies the child-like needs still present in the adult.) This identification is so strong that Freud goes on to suggest, "the precondition for enjoyment" of neurotic characters is that "the spectator shall also be neurotic" (p. 147). Because non-neurotic spectators will simply reject a neurotic character if that is the only way the character is presented to them, it is important that dramatists show the process through which a normal character becomes neurotic, not just the end result, so that even non-neurotic spectators have something with which to empathize.

Despite the existing connections between theatre and psychoanalysis, "performance theorists [as opposed to literary drama critics and psychoanalysts] first became interested in psychoanalysis . . . because of its attention to the process of identity formation, especially the formation of gender roles" (Carlson, *Performance*, p. 50). Feminist performance theorists have made extensive use of psychoanalytical theory, frequently in ways that simultaneously exploit it and critique it. Although it should be noted that a great deal of the influence of psychoanalytical theory on performance studies came by way of the revisionist psychoanalyst Jacques LACAN rather than directly from Freud, psychoanalytical thought, like Marxian political theory, is deeply ensconced in the field's bedrock. The essays collected in Patrick Campbell and Adrian Kear's *Psychoanalysis and Performance* (2001) demonstrate a renewed interest in Freud on the part of a number of the field's most important scholars.

Further reading

By Freud

An Outline of Psycho-Analysis. Translated by James Strachey. New York: W.W. Norton, 1949.

Civilization and its Discontents. Translated by James Strachey. New York: W.W. Norton, 1961.

The Future of an Illusion. In *The Standard Edition*, XXI. London: Hogarth Press, 1953–74.

The Interpretation of Dreams, First Part. In *The Standard Edition*, IV. London: Hogarth Press, 1953–74.

Introductory Lectures on Psycho-Analysis. In *The Standard Edition*, XV–XVI. London: Hogarth Press, 1953–74.

*"Psychopathic Characters on the Stage." Translated by Henry Alden Bunker. *The Tulane Drama Review* 4, no. 3 (1960): 144–48.

*"Two Encyclopedia Articles." In *The Standard Edition*, XVIII. Edited and translated by James Strachey in collaboration with Anna Freud. London: Hogarth Press, 1953–74.

"The Uncanny." In *The Standard Edition*, XVII. London: Hogarth Press, 1953–74.

About Freud

*Campbell, Patrick and Kear, Adrian (eds). *Psychoanalysis and Performance*. London: Routledge, 2001.

Carlson, Marvin. *Performance: A Critical Introduction*, 2nd edn. New York: Routledge, 2004.

Diamond, Elin. "Realism's Hysteria: Disruptions in the Theatre of Knowledge." In *Unmaking Mimesis: Essays on Feminism and Theatre*. London: Routledge, 1997.

*Gay, Peter. *Freud: A Life for our Times*. New York: W.W. Norton, 1988.

Gunn, Joshua. "Mourning Speech: Haunting and the Spectral Voices of Nine-Eleven." *Text and Performance Quarterly* 24, no. 2 (2004): 91–114.

McDougall, Gordon. "Theatre and the Unconscious: The Three-Dimensional Dream." *Studies in Theatre and Performance* 23, no. 2 (2003): 107–16.

Neuringer, Charles. "Freud and the Theatre." *Journal of the American Academy of Psychoanalysis* 20 (1992): 142–48.

Pellegrini, Ann. *Performance Anxieties: Staging Psychoanalysis, Staging Race*. London: Routledge, 1996.

Ricoeur, Paul. *Freud and Philosophy: An Essay on Interpretation*. Translated by Denis Savage. New Haven, CT: Yale University Press, 1970.

Rokem, Freddie. "Acting and Psychoanalysis: Street Scenes, Private Scenes, and Transference." *Theatre Journal* 39, no. 2 (1987): 175–84.

Sander, Fred M. "Psychoanalysis, Drama, and the Family: The Ever-Widening Scope." *Annual of Psychoanalysis* 29 (2001): 279–99.

Sievers, David W. *Freud on Broadway: A History of Psychoanalysis and the American Drama*. New York: Hermitage, 1955.

2   Karl Marx

Key concepts

- historical materialism
- dialectic
- mode of production (relations and forces)
- proletariat, capitalists, bourgeoisie
- means of production
- base, superstructure
- alienation
- ideology

Karl Marx (1818–83) was a German political philosopher. He was born in Trier, Germany to liberal Jewish parents who had become Protestant in order to advance the law career of his father. In 1836, after a year at the University of Bonn, he entered the University of Berlin, where he concentrated on philosophy. Deeply influenced by Hegelian thought, he was a member of a student group known as the Young Hegelians who espoused a radical, atheistic version of Hegel's dialectic.

Marx's doctoral thesis on Greek philosophy was accepted in 1841. Unable to find a university position, he became a journalist for the liberal newspaper the *Rhenish Gazette*. He wrote articles on a wide range of topics, touching especially on political and social concerns, and served briefly as the paper's editor before it was censored by the Prussian government for, among other things, articles about worker conditions.

In 1843, Marx, newly married, moved to Paris to take a position as co-editor of a new publication, the *German-French Annals*. This journal expressed communist ideas and failed to draw the interest of the French. Deemed subversive by the Prussian government, the publication was confiscated and its editors sought for arrest. Once again unemployed and now unable to return to Germany, Marx devoted his energy to writing a work of political philosophy that would express his socialist views. At this time (1844), Marx befriended Friedrich Engels (1820–95), socialist son of a German industrialist, who became Marx's lifelong collaborator and benefactor.

At the insistence of the Prussian government, the French expelled Marx and other German communists from Paris. Marx moved to Brussels, supported financially by Engels. In 1847, Marx and Engels attended the Congress of the Communist League in London where Marx asserted his views on how to bring about a communist revolution. As a result, he and Engels were commissioned to articulate the League's working doctrines. This commission led to the publication of *The Communist Manifesto* (published in German in 1848).

After the 1848 French revolution, Marx moved first to Paris, then to Cologne, back to Paris as conservative factions regained control of Germany, and then, late in the summer of 1849, to London, where he remained throughout the rest of his life. Marx lived in poverty for a time, but with Engels' support and his own family inheritances, he eventually enjoyed a comfortable lifestyle in London with his family. He continued to organize social movements and to write. In 1852, and continuing for ten years, he became a regular contributor to the *New York Tribune*. Marx published the first volume of *Capital*, a critique of capitalist economics, in German in 1867. *Capital* brought attention to Marx's ideas and a second edition was published in 1871. Translations into other languages soon followed, though an English translation did not appear until after Marx's death. Two subsequent volumes of *Capital* remained unfinished at Marx's death and were completed later by Engels.

Marxism, or Marxist theory, is based on ideas formulated by Marx and Engels as a critique of industrial capitalism. It focuses attention on social history in relation to political economy, especially class struggle. From a Marxist perspective, history is not driven by ideas, values, or some overarching spirit. Rather, it is a record of struggle, rooted in material existence, for food, shelter, products of labor, and control over the means of production. Marx's ideas – disseminated, in part, through various interpretations of and elaborations on Marxism – have had a tremendous impact on twentieth-century politics as well as on critical theory, literary theory, cultural studies, history, sociology, economics, the arts, and philosophy.

We can conceive of Marxist theory in at least two ways. First, Marxist theory is a revolutionary critique of capitalist society. Marx was personally concerned with the need for social change in light of what he saw as the injustice and oppression caused by nineteenth-century industrial capitalism and the economic relations it engendered. His analysis of how industrial capitalism operated and how it caused oppression was directed at changing this system and thereby ending the human suffering that it produced. Second, and more importantly for our purposes, Marxist theory is a way to analyze not only economic relations but also those values and viewpoints created by industrial capitalism that impact ostensibly non-political endeavors such as literature, the arts, and other cultural products and practices. Marxist theory underscores the ideological nature of all human enterprises.

Central to Marxist thought is Marx's philosophy of history. Known as **historical materialism,** it views historical change as the result of the actions of human beings within the material world, and not as the hand of God or some other extra-human or spiritual force. In this materialist view of history, Marx was influenced by Ludwig Feuerbach (1804–72), who emphasized the material conditions of the world and was critical of the idealism of Hegelian thinking, which stressed ideas and the spiritual nature of the universe and historical change. For Marx, what propels history is a **dialectic** expressing economic and other conflicts between social classes. Hegel, too, had understood history as dialectical, with change taking place as a series of successive movements from thesis to antithesis to synthesis. But whereas Hegel saw this as a history of the human spirit, Marx saw it as a history of human struggle over material goods and their production. This is why Marx is said to have stood Hegel on his head. Material circumstances shape ideas, not vice versa.

Marxism describes the historical development of different **modes of production,** a concept referring to the ways societies organize economic relations in order to allow for the production of goods. The Marxist characterization of capitalism as an oppressive and unjust system of labor and production centers on social relations and the tools used in the production of goods. Labor is not performed in isolation but within larger human networks. Human patterns of economic organization, or **relations of production,** interact with human labor and technologies, or **forces of production,** to create the mode of production.

Modes of production differ across historical periods. Marxist cultural analysis is especially focused on industrial capitalism, viewing it as an economic system that promotes an unequal and therefore unjust mode of production. Marx's discussion of class struggle in capitalist society predicates that economic development progresses from primitive to feudal to capitalist, and that class struggle corresponds to the dominant mode of production in each society. It is only with the development of a socialist mode of production that class distinctions and conflicts end. Historical change can occur only within the context of dialectical conflicts between classes. Contradictions between those in control and those controlled inevitably lead to class conflict. It is the dialectic of class confrontations that engenders a new society. The ultimate goal, of course, is a socialist, classless state.

In a capitalist mode of production, the relations of production are such that workers labor to turn raw material into finished goods and owners control the sale and distribution of these products, collecting their surplus value. Such a system, says Marx, inevitably results in creation of class distinctions in which the **proletariat** – workers who sell their labor power for a wage in order to make a living – enables the **capitalists** who own and control the **means of production** (that is, the natural resources, factories, machines, and other material resources) to recover a profit at the expense of the workers. A third class, the **bourgeoisie,** are neither owners nor workers, but service providers such as teachers and doctors. Although they provide services to both other classes, they are usually identified as having the same class as capitalists.

For Marx, economic organization – that is, modes of production – shape other aspects of society. The concepts of **base** and **superstructure** explain this relationship. Base refers to a society's economic mode of production, which determines its superstructure, that is, its political, social, religious, artistic, moral, scientific, and other cultural productions. From this perspective, art, for instance, is not an independent or autonomous mode of human activity but is conditioned and determined by a society's mode of production and the relations of production it engenders. This is a materialist theory of art, viewing it as part of a society's superstructure.

The economic base is supported by a superstructure that justifies the base and seeks to naturalize class differences as an overarching reality that people have no possibility of changing. Such a system is understood by Marxism as fundamentally exploitative and changeable only through the dialectical struggle between classes. Struggle occurs because the inequities and contradictions of an unequal system become evident over time. Marxism forecasts that the dialectical struggle will eventually destroy capitalism and establish a class-free socialism in its place. This event will mark the end of history in the sense that further economic change will no longer occur because unequal class relations that fueled the dialectical struggle have ceased to exist.

Marxism draws attention to processes of **alienation**, especially through the stratification of society into different social classes, where upper classes have privileged access to the goods produced by the lower classes. Alienation – a result of unequal class relations caused by a capitalist mode of production – occurs in two ways. First, a capitalist mode of production is a system in which workers produce goods from which only capitalist owners profit. This is labor alienated from its own efforts. Second, workers are alienated from themselves in a capitalist system. According to Marx, this occurs because workers become commodities when they must sell their alienated labor in the marketplace, just as other goods are sold. Thus, workers are alienated from their own humanity.

Marxist theory conceives of **ideology** as a false consciousness that distorts social and material reality, functioning to keep people in their place within the capitalist system. This distortion prevents people from viewing relations of production as they really are. Therefore ideology is an aspect of superstructure: it is produced by the economic base and functions to legitimize that base. Ideologies determine what can be thought and believed about politics, religion, literature, and other aspects of culture. But ideologies are not autonomous; they depend, says Marx, on the prevailing economic mode of production and serve as a justification for its continued existence. The Protestant work ethic, for instance, promoted the value of hard work and profit-making without desire for personal profit or gain. This way of working was understood to be the will of God. Thus, profit-seeking was equated with religious duty. From a Marxist perspective, the Protestant work ethic exemplifies an ideology that legitimizes an economic mode of production which requires workers to toil long hours under difficult working conditions. The laborer who espouses this work ethic falsely understands his or her hard work as freely choosing to follow the will of God, but such a view is in fact a distortion of reality, promoting a mode of production that oppresses workers in order to benefit capitalist owners. There is the illusion of choice or free will when in fact there is none.

In introductory material for the landmark anthology *Critical Theory and Performance*, Janelle Reinelt notes, "Marxist language can be found all through this book: ideology, hegemony, economism, surplus value, commodification, reification – all these and several other terms have become useful to cultural studies critics, to historians, to psychoanalysts, to feminists" ("Introduction," p. 161). Reinelt points here to the way that Marxist ideas and language have infiltrated the humanities, to the degree that Marxian ideas are part of the ground on which a discipline such as performance studies was built. Frequently, Marxian ideas are in play, particularly in materialist analyses of many stripes, even when Marx himself is not directly under discussion.

Marx's relevance to performance studies has three aspects: his impact on performance theory and practice, primarily through the German playwright and director Bertolt Brecht (1898–1956); his influence on the materialist strain of performance studies; and his own use of dramatic and theatrical concepts in his writing. As this is not the place for an extended discussion of Brecht's work as both a theorist and practitioner of theatre, it will have to be sufficient to say that Brecht was the most important figure to address the question of what a Marxist aesthetic might mean for the theatre. Brecht's approach to the question of how theatre might be used to advance social change remains paradigmatic and has been addressed by performance theorists focused more on gender and other social categories than on class (see Diamond).

Because Raymond WILLIAMS was among the most prominent of Marxist critics to take an interest in theatre and drama, examples of materialist analysis of performance and the processes through which it is created can be found in the bibliography at the end of his entry in this volume. Another interesting issue to consider in relation to performance studies is Marx's own use of implicitly and explicitly theatrical metaphors in describing some of his central concepts, including revolution and commodity production. In *The Eighteenth Brumaire of Louis Bonaparte* (1852), Marx famously corrected Hegel's comment that important historical events repeat themselves by adding, "the first time as tragedy, the second as farce" (*The Portable Karl Marx*, p. 287), and Martin Puchner has pointed out the dialogic and theatrical qualities of *The Communist Manifesto* ("Manifesto = Theatre," pp. 462–63). But Puchner, Alice Rayner, and Andrew Parker all show, albeit in different contexts, that Marx treated theatricality as a negative quantity. For Marx, the difference between *being* and *seeming* was crucial: being was the realm of material human reality (such as labor and use value), while seeming was that of ideology, the commodity, and exchange value. In his revolutionary rhetoric, Marx consistently assigned acting, performance, and theatricality to the realm of seeming.

Further reading

By Marx

Karl Marx: A Reader. Edited by Jon Elster. Cambridge: Cambridge University Press, 1986.

*Karl Marx: Selected Writings. Edited by David McLellan, 2nd edn. Oxford: Oxford University Press, 2000.

The Marx-Engels Reader. Edited by Robert C. Tucker, 2nd edn. New York: W.W. Norton, 1978.

The Portable Karl Marx. Edited by Eugene Kamenka. New York: Penguin, 1983.

About Marx

Blau, Herbert. *To All Appearances: Ideology and Performance*. New York: Routledge, 1992.

Brecht, Bertolt. *Brecht on Theatre: The Development of an Aesthetic*. Edited and translated by John Willett. New York: Hill & Wang, 1964.

Carver, Terrell (ed.). *The Cambridge Companion to Marx*. Cambridge: Cambridge University Press, 1992.

Derrida, Jacques. "Injunction of Marx." In *Specters of Marx: The State of the Debt, the Work of Mourning, and the New International*. Translated by Peggy Kamuf. London: Routledge, 1994.

Diamond, Elin. "Brechtian Theory / Feminist Theory: Toward a Gestic Feminist Criticism." In *Performance: Critical Concepts*, Vol. III. Edited by Philip Auslander. London: Routledge, 2003. Originally published in *TDR: Journal of Performance Studies* 32, no. 1 (1988): 82–94.

Elster, Jon. *Making Sense of Marx*. Cambridge: Cambridge University Press, 1985.

Joseph, Miranda. "The Performance of Production and Consumption." In *Performance: Critical Concepts*, Vol. III. Edited by Philip Auslander. London: Routledge, 2003. Originally published in *Social Text* 16, no. 1 (1998): 25–62.

**McLellan, David. *Karl Marx: His Life and Thought*. New York: Harper & Row, 1973.

Parker, Andrew. "Unthinking Sex: Marx, Engels and the Scene of Writing." *Social Text* 29 (1991): 28–45.

Puchner, Martin. "Manifesto = Theatre." *Theatre Journal* 54, no. 3 (2002): 449–65.

Rayner, Alice. "Rude Mechanicals and the *Specters of Marx*." *Theatre Journal* 54, no. 4 (2002): 535–54.

Reinelt, Janelle. "Introduction: After Marx." In *Critical Theory and Performance*. Edited by Janelle Reinelt and Joseph Roach. Ann Arbor, MI: University of Michigan Press, 1995.

Singer, Peter. *Marx: A Very Short Introduction*. Oxford: Oxford University Press, 2000.

Wolff, Jonathan. *Why Read Marx Today?* Oxford: Oxford University Press, 2002.

3 Friedrich Nietzsche

Key concepts

- power
- good, bad, and evil
- slave morality
- death of God
- overman
- Dionysian, Apollonian

Friedrich Wilhelm Nietzsche (1844–1900) was born in Röcken, Prussia. He was the eldest of three children. His father and both grandfathers were ordained ministers in the Lutheran Church, and early on he seemed destined for the ministry (other children called him "little pastor"). His father died at 36, when Friedrich was only 5. About five months later his baby brother Joseph also died and was buried with his father, wrapped in his arms.

Nietzsche received an excellent education. From 14 to 19 he studied at Schulpforta, an elite boarding school. In 1864 he entered the University of Bonn to study theology and philology, but a year later moved to the University of Leipzig to focus exclusively on philology. In 1867 he took leave of his studies to serve for a year in the Prussian military as an officer in the horse-drawn artillery. In 1869, at 24, he was appointed professor of classical philology at the University of Basel. At the time of his appointment he had yet to complete his exams and dissertation, but the University of Leipzig waived those requirements and awarded him the doctoral degree. In 1870 he took leave from the university to serve as a medic in the Franco-Prussian war, but was discharged within months due to a serious illness.

As a result of failing health, Nietzsche took leave of his professorate in 1876, and then resigned in 1879. Having given up his Prussian citizenship without being granted Swiss citizenship, he remained "stateless" for the rest of his life. For the next ten years, he wrote prolifically while traveling and visiting friends throughout Europe and elsewhere.

In January 1889, while in Turin, he suffered a mental breakdown from which he never recovered. The story goes that he collapsed after wrapping his arms around the neck of a horse which had just been brutally whipped by a coachman. After a year in a sanitarium in Jena, he lived with his mother until her death in 1897, and then spent his last years with his sister, Elizabeth, a devout anti-Semite who published *The Will to Power* (based on his 1880s notebooks) and who later brought Nietzsche's works to the attention of influential Nazis, including Hitler, and Mussolini. In fact, although there are certain passages in his writings that easily support the anti-Jewish ideology of the Nazis, Nietzsche hated German nationalism and expressed much alienation from his sister on account of her anti-Semitism.

Nietzsche described his work as philosophizing "with a hammer." Trained in classical philology, he is best known as a critic of prevailing western European cultural values. In particular, he challenged the Christian foundations of those values. But his philosophy was not simply negative or destructive, as some unfairly represent it. On the contrary, his critical eye on western civilization was inspired by the desire to affirm what he understood to be the source of life – a kind of primordial, creative energy beyond rationality and beyond moral categorization as good or evil. He believed that western civilization was in decline because it had drained that life force, ceding power and authority to those who fear it.

Nietzsche conceived of the world as a turbulent sea of non-rational forces that are both destructive and generative. Contrary to the predominant Christian worldview of his time, Nietzsche saw the world not as a moral universe, created and managed by a moral God, but as a chaotic "monster of energy" in which humans live and move and have their being. **Power,** therefore, must be understood not as an object to be held but a never-ending struggle within this ever-changing sea of forces. Life, therefore, is driven by a will to power that is antecedent to morality.

Of particular importance to contemporary thought is Nietzsche's *On the Genealogy of Morals* (1887), which explores the origins of contemporary moral categories of **good, bad, and evil**. He argues that these categories are not essential or universal categories but are culturally constructed through operations of social power through history. Goodness is simply that which is valued by those in power, and badness is its opposite, either as a threat to their power (e.g. enemies) or as the antithesis of it (e.g. the weak). In the earliest stages of human history, Nietzsche argues, the good and the bad were determined by the dominant knightly-aristocratic class. That which furthered their health and happiness in the world was good; that which did not was bad. Then came moralistic religion, the champions of which Nietzsche calls the priestly-aristocratic class. Whereas the knightly-aristocratic values were based on this-worldly physical pleasure and the furtherance of life, the priestly-aristocratic values were just the opposite, glorifying selflessness and weakness, and calling the knightly-aristocratic affirmation of life and health not just bad but downright "evil." Against them, the priestly-aristocratic class has established a **slave morality** that glorifies weakness and makes people feel badly for all that comes naturally, that is, for their will to power, pleasure, and the enjoyment of life.

Historians and anthropologists would rightly doubt Nietzsche's provocative if also simplistic history of society as he presents it in *Genealogy*. The importance of this work for contemporary thought, however, lies in his genealogical approach. Instead of seeing ideas and values like "evil" as universal truths or divine revelations, he approaches them as products of history that take form over time through ongoing social struggle. They are, in short, effects of power. This way of thinking had a profound influence on Michel FOUCAULT, who took up the idea of genealogy explicitly, as well as such other important figures as Georges BATAILLE, Judith BUTLER, Gilles DELEUZE, Luce IRIGARAY, and Jean-François LYOTARD.

When Nietzsche pronounces the **death of God** in *The Gay Science* (1882; section 125) and the Prologue to *Thus Spoke Zarathustra* (1883–85), it is important to understand his meaning. He is not calling for or celebrating the death of God, but is describing what he sees as a fact of modern western civilization, namely that it no longer lives by faith in "God" as a monolithic, ultimate author and guarantor of moral law who sees into the hearts of all people and will judge them accordingly. For Nietzsche, the most important thing about the death of God is what must die with him, namely, the Christian conceptions of human sinfulness, fallenness, and indebtedness. Nietzsche's interest in making this pronouncement is to free people from bondage to a slave morality according to which life is lived in hopes of some future, otherworldly reward. We see this most clearly, perhaps, in his Prologue of *Thus Spoke Zarathustra*. Zarathustra, the hero of exuberant freedom and affirmation of life on earth, meets a saint in the forest. Whereas Zarathustra loves the earth and human beings, the saint has given up on humans and seeks only to love God. As the saint departs, Zarathustra wonders to himself, "Could it be possible? This old saint in the forest has not yet heard anything of this, that *God is dead*!" (p. 12). Immediately following this interchange with the old saint, Zarathustra begins preaching the coming of the **overman** (*Übermensch*, often translated as "superman"), that is, the human being who has overcome the Christian notion of human nature as fallen and sinful and the slave morality that goes with it.

Nietzsche's first book, *The Birth of Tragedy* (published in German in 1872) has long been considered a canonical work of dramatic theory. It describes the creative, primordial life force as **Dionysian**, after the ancient gender-bending god of wine, masquerade, violence, and orgy. Contrary to the prevailing view of ancient Greece as a world of noble harmony and rational order, Nietzsche argued that Greek culture existed in the tension between two opposing forces: on the one hand, the **Apollonian** forces of moral order and sober rationality; on the other hand, the Dionysian forces of amoral desire and non-rational, creative exuberance. The Apollonian is order; the Dionysian is primordial, that is, the chaotic life force that precedes the order of civilization and is its creative source. Nietzsche believed that in the centuries since ancient Greece, western civilization had gradually repressed the Dionysian, leaving modern western society predominantly Apollonian, starved of creative energy and in poor health. Therefore he called for a resurrection of the Dionysian, and looked to the German music and art of his time, particularly the operatic *Gesamtkunstwerke* of the composer Richard Wagner, as a potential means to the rebirth of the tragic spirit.

Even in *The Birth of Tragedy*, however, Nietzsche raises some doubts about whether this spirit could be reborn in modern times. These doubts center to a large extent on the contemporary audience, which he accuses of being "critics," whose education and socialization have rendered them incapable of Dionysian surrender to music, rather than true "aesthetic listeners" (section 22). In later writings, Nietzsche seemed to become more and more hostile to the performing arts, describing himself, at one point, as "essentially anti-theatrical." This was in *Nietzsche Contra Wagner* (1888), a text Nietzsche produced by juxtaposing passages from his earlier writings, sometimes revising them. There, he condemns theatre as a "mass art" that caters to the lowest common denominator and degrades its audience: "In the theatre, one becomes people, herd female, pharisee, voting cattle, patron, idiot . . . [E]ven the most powerful conscience is vanquished by the leveling magic of the great number . . . [O]ne becomes a mere neighbor" (pp. 665–66). He thus suggests that theatre inculcates a slave morality in its audience. He further argues that only art which demands no audience but is produced and appreciated in solitude is of value: "whatever is perfect suffers no witnesses" (p. 665).

Taken together, Nietzsche's writings on theatre and music seem contradictory: one the one hand, he celebrates musical drama as a form in which the Dionysian spirit could be reborn, while on the other saying how much he despises the theatre. Nietzsche himself claimed to have changed his mind about Wagner (and perhaps he did), but one should hesitate before accepting anything at face value from this playful and elusive writer. As Christopher Morris reminds us, however opposed to theatricality Nietzsche may have claimed to be, his texts are frequently multivocal and dialogical ("'Alienated from his Own Being'"). *Nietzsche Contra Wagner*, for example, bears the melodramatic subtitle "Out of the Files of a Psychologist." Implicitly, there are at least two characters involved, one a recovering Wagner addict (one section is entitled "How I Broke Away from Wagner"), the other a psychologist studying his case. It becomes distinctly possible, then, that Nietzsche is not speaking "as himself" when railing against the theatre but is using a character as a mouthpiece for a point of view. Jon McKenzie's analysis of these tensions is helpful to those pondering Nietzsche's relationship to performance studies: "this play we find in Nietzsche, between the theatrical and antitheatrical, may very well mark the rupture of performance into modern thought, the emergence of performance as a problem, a site of contestation" (p. 122).

Further reading

By Nietzsche

Beyond Good and Evil. Translated by Walter Kaufmann. New York: Random House, 1966.

*The Birth of Tragedy and *The Case of Wagner.* Translated by Walter Kaufmann. New York: Random House, 1967.

Daybreak: Thoughts on the Prejudices of Morality. Translated by R.J. Hollingdale. Cambridge: Cambridge University Press, 1982.

The Gay Science, with a Prelude of Rhymes and an Appendix of Songs. Translated by Walter Kaufmann. New York: Random House, 1974.

Nietzsche Contra Wagner. In *The Portable Nietzsche.* Translated by Walter Kaufmann. New York: Penguin, 1954.

*On the Genealogy of Morals and *Ecce Homo.* Translated by Walter Kaufmann and R.J. Hollingdale. New York: Random House, 1967.

*Thus Spoke Zarathustra. Translated by Walter Kaufmann. New York: Viking, 1968.

The Will to Power. Translated by Walter Kaufmann. New York: Random House, 1967.

About Nietzsche

Bataille, Georges. *On Nietzsche.* Translated by Bruce Boone. London: Athlone Press, 1992.

Kaufmann, Walter. *Nietzsche: Philosopher, Psychologist, Antichrist.* Princeton, NJ: Princeton University Press, 1950.

Leavell, Linda. "Nietzsche's Theory of Tragedy in the Plays of T.S. Eliot." *Twentieth Century Literature* 31, no. 1 (1985): 111–26.

McKenzie, Jon. "Democracy's Performance." *The Drama Review* 47, no. 2 (2003): 117–28.

*Morris, Christopher. "'Alienated from his Own Being': Nietzsche, Bayreuth and the Problem of Identity." *Journal of the Royal Musical Association*, 127 (2002): 44–71.

*Nehamas, Alexander. *Nietzsche: Life as Literature.* Cambridge, MA: Harvard University Press, 1985.

Puchner, Martin. "The Theater in Modernist Thought." *New Literary History*, 33 (2002): 521–32.

4   Ferdinand de Saussure

Key concepts

- structural linguistics, structuralism
- semiology, semiotics
- langue, parole
- synchronic, diachronic
- sign (signifier and signified)
- arbitrariness of the sign
- binary opposition (meaning as difference)

Ferdinand de Saussure (1857–1913) was a Swiss linguist whose posthumously published *Course in General Linguistics* (1916) became a catalyst for the development of structuralism. Saussure was born in Geneva, Switzerland, into a family with a lineage of noted academics going back to the eighteenth century. Saussure himself displayed a gift for languages from an early age. At the University of Geneva, he studied not only linguistics but also theology, law, and chemistry. In 1878, at 21 years old, he published *Memoir on the Original System of Vowels in the Indo-European Languages*, a comparative study of vowel usage in proto-Indo-European languages.

Saussure received his doctorate from the University of Leipzig in 1880. From 1881 to 1891 he taught linguistics at the École des hautes études in Paris. In 1891, he returned to the University of Geneva where he taught courses on Sanskrit and general linguistics for the remainder of his career. Although he published very little, his students at the University of Geneva compiled and transcribed their notes from his general linguistics course lectures and had them published in 1916 under the title *Course in General Linguistics*.

As detailed in *Course in General Linguistics*, Saussure's perspective on language has impacted many fields of academic inquiry including literature, philosophy, anthropology, and psychology. In the work of influential twentieth-century critical theorists – such as Michel FOUCAULT, Louis ALTHUSSER, Roland BARTHES, Claude Lévi-Strauss, Jacques LACAN, Julia KRISTEVA, and Jacques DERRIDA – Saussure's assertion that linguistic meaning resides in the relationships between words has constituted a critical point of departure. Saussure's philosophy of language is commonly referred to as **structural linguistics** since its strategy for examining language and meaning centers on investigating structures within a system. In concert with the work of Martin Heidegger and other philosophers of being, **structuralism** brought about a major shift in twentieth-century thought often referred to as the "linguistic turn," which has become shorthand for the conviction that meaning does not exist outside language.

In *Course in General Linguistics*, Saussure advocates the scientific study of language which, for him, concerns "the life of signs within society." This method contrasts with historical linguistics as then practiced by European philologists who sought to trace Indo-European languages back to a common origin. Saussure called his new linguistic science **"semiology,"** a term derived from the Greek word for "sign" (*semeîon*). Semiology, also called **semiotics**, is the science of signs, that is, the study of the structure of language as a system of signification rather than the history of language.

In order to study language as a system of signs, Saussure makes a distinction between **langue** and **parole**. *Langue* ("language") refers to language as a structured system operating at a particular time and place, and to the linguistic rules that determine how a language can be used in practice. In contrast, *parole* ("speech") refers to particular instances of speech within the system. Without *langue*, *parole* – what individuals say – would be impossible. For Saussure, the object of inquiry, then, is *langue*, which constitutes overarching linguistic system that makes specific utterances possible.

As the terms *langue* and *parole* suggest, the study of language as a system requires a **synchronic** ("at the same time") rather than a **diachronic** ("through time") approach. Synchrony refers to the study of language – especially spoken language – as it is used at a particular moment in time. Diachrony refers to the study of language over time. Nineteenth-century philology employed a diachronic methodology that derived from a central assumption that language could be comprehended only through a study of its historical changes. Thus, if a word could be traced back to its origin, then the path to its present meaning could be followed.

Saussure advocates a synchronic approach to language as a system, asserting that language can be understood only in terms of relationship. Instead of etymology as the conveyor of a word's meaning, Saussure argues that meaning is produced by a word's relationship to other words occurring at a particular time, within a particular system of relationships. Thus, for instance, the contemporary word "dog" means something not because of its historical derivation from the Middle English *dogge*, which is in turn derived from the Old English *docga*, but rather because of the current relationship of "dog" to other words like "puppy" and "cat." In Saussure's analysis, all of these terms are part of a system, and their meanings and significances derive from relationships with other signs within that system.

As illustrated by the previous example, a central claim made by Saussure's synchronic linguistic analysis is that words do not have inherent meaning. Instead, meaning resides in relationships of difference and similarity within a larger linguistic system – words are not units of self-contained meaning. A related concern – whether language is natural or conventional – also plays an important role in Saussure's linguistic analysis. A natural view of language proposes that language names things in the world because there is some intrinsic relationship between a word and the thing named. By contrast, if language is conventional, both concrete things and abstract concepts are named on the basis of an arbitrary decision to use a certain sound to represent a certain idea. As we will see, Saussure develops a theory of language that clearly sides with the idea of language as conventional.

How does Saussure arrive at the conclusion that language is primarily conventional? He starts with the idea of the linguistic **sign**. A sign may be a word or some other form. Regardless of its particular form, however, every sign consists of a **signifier** and a **signified**.

$$sign = \frac{signifier}{signified}$$

A linguistic sign comprises a sound-image, such as the letters d-o-g spoken or written (the signifier) and the object or concept associated with the sound-image (the signified). What determines the signification (i.e. meaning) of a sign is not its sound-image or linguistic origin, but its place within the larger network of interrelationships – that is, within the larger linguistic structure. Thus a structuralist approach focuses on the relationship of individual parts to the larger whole – the structure – within which significance is determined.

One of Saussure's key insights, then, is that the sign is fundamentally relational. Further, the relationship between the signifier and the signified is **arbitrary**. That is, any signifier can potentially stand for any signified. The fact that *dog* signifies a four-legged domestic animal in English, while *chien* and *inu* point to this same animal in French and Japanese respectively, is evidence that there is no necessary relationship between the letters d-o-g and a common pet. The word *dog* is an arbitrary designation. We could call dogs by some other term as long as we agree culturally on that usage. There is no particular dog designated by the word, nor is there some inherent quality ("dogness") contained in or conveyed by the sound-image *dog*.

Since signs are arbitrary, the meaning of any particular sign is determined in terms of similarity and difference in relation to other signs. Thus, meaning is founded on **binary oppositions**, such as light/dark, good/bad, inside/outside, margin/center, male/female, positive/negative, immanent/transcendent, life/death, sacred/profane, etc. Within these binary pairs, the meaning of one is basically the opposite of the other. Meaning, then, is predicated on difference. Sacred means "not profane," inside means "not outside," and so on. Saussure argues that

> In language there are only differences. Even more important: a difference generally implies positive terms between which the difference is set up; but in language there are only differences *without positive terms*. Whether we take the signified or the signifier, language has neither ideas nor sounds that existed before the linguistic system, but only conceptual and phonic differences that have issued from the system. The idea or phonic substance that a sign contains is of less importance than the other signs that surround it.
>
> (Saussure, *Course in General Linguistics*, p. 120)

Although Saussure has had a significant impact on theatre and performance studies through his influence on the theorists mentioned above, his insights into the structure of language have also influenced theatre and performance studies more directly through various attempts to formulate a semiotics of theatre. These began in the 1930s with the Prague School of structuralist semioticians (see Deak), but flourished during a period from the early 1970s through the early 1980s when a host of European and American performance theorists took up the semiological project. (See Alter, and Pavis, *Analyzing Performance*, for brief discussions of the evolution of theatrical semiotics.) But the theoretical tide turned against semiotics, in part because it seemed impossible to reduce theatrical representation, which includes the bodies of actors and spectators as well as both linguistic and pictorial representations, to a linguistically modeled system of signs and codes. Culturally oriented theorists also came to resist Saussure's schema as well; Raymond WILLIAMS, for one, argues that Saussure's claim that the relationship between signifier and signified is arbitrary deprives social participants of agency. For Williams, language is created by people, in particular historical and social circumstances, and the ways it reflects those concrete circumstances are not arbitrary (see Moriarity, especially pp. 59–65).

It is also the case, as Marvin Carlson points out, that theatrical semiotics was caught in the crossfire as performance studies sought to establish itself as a discipline apart from theatre studies:

> An important concern among performance theorists in the early days of the field's development was to show how performance differed from theatre, and for many, the association of theatre with discursivity, structure, absence and semiotics and of performance with libidinal flow, presence, and poststructuralism provided a convenient and useful means for doing this. Thus semiotic theory, while it remained an inescapable element in the intellectual background of modern performance theory, became, consciously or unconsciously, more and more excluded from the further development of that theory.
>
> (Carlson, *Performance*, p. 57)

The ultimate inescapability of semiotics is demonstrated, however, by the development within performance studies of performance analysis, which is, at its heart, a semiotic enterprise. Theorists of performance analysis try to develop schemas able to address more aspects of performance and its reception by an audience than classical semiotics, but in less rigidly systematic ways. One of the key figures in the evolution of performance analysis out of theatrical semiotics is the French scholar Patrice Pavis.

Further reading

By Saussure
Course in General Linguistics. Translated by Wade Baskin. New York: McGraw-Hill, 1959.

About Saussure

Alter, Jean. "Theatre Semiotics at a Crossroads: On a Book by Patrice Pavis." *Boundary 2* 18, no. 1 (1991): 238–53.

Aston, Elaine. *Theatre as Sign-System: A Semiotics of Text and Performance*. London: Routledge, 1992.

Belsey, Catherine. *Poststructuralism: A Very Short Introduction*. Oxford: Oxford University Press, 2002.

Bennett, Susan. *Theatre Audiences: A Theory of Production and Reception*. London: Routledge, 1998.

Carlson, Marvin. *Performance: A Critical Introduction*, 2nd edn. New York: Routledge, 2004.

*Culler, Jonathan. *Ferdinand de Saussure*, revised edn. Ithaca, NY: Cornell University Press, 1986.

Culler, Jonathan. *The Pursuit of Signs: Semiotics, Literature, Deconstruction*. Ithaca, NY: Cornell University Press, 1981.

Deak, Frantisek. "Structuralism in the Theatre: The Prague School Contribution." *The Drama Review* 20, no. 4 (1976): 83–94.

*Elam, Keir. *The Semiotics of Theatre and Drama*, 2nd edn. London: Routledge, 2002.

Fischer-Lichte, Erika. *The Semiotics of Theatre*. Translated by Jeremy Gaines and Doris L. Jones. Bloomington, IN: Indiana University Press, 1992.

Lévi-Strauss, Claude. "The Structural Study of Myth." In *Structural Anthropology*. Translated by Claire Jacobson and Brooke Grundfest Schoepf. New York: Basic Books, 1963.

Moriarity, Michael. "The Longest Cultural Journey: Raymond Williams and French Theory." *Social Text* 30 (1992): 57–77.

Oswald, Laura. "Towards a Semiotics of Performance: Staging the Double in Genet." *Poetics Today* 8, no. 2 (1987): 261–83.

*Pavis, Patrice. *Analyzing Performance: Theater, Dance and Film*. Translated by David Williams. Ann Arbor, MI: University of Michigan Press, 2003.

Pavis, Patrice. *Languages of the Stage: Essays in the Semiology of the Theatre*. New York: PAJ Publications, 1983.

Part II
The theorists

5 Louis Althusser

Key concepts

- base, superstructure
- practices
- ideology
- Repressive State Apparatuses
- Ideological State Apparatuses
- interpellation

Louis Althusser (1918–90) was a French Marxist political philosopher. He was born in Algeria and educated in Algiers and France. He was admitted to the École normale supérieure in 1939, but World War II disrupted his studies when he was called to military duty. During the German occupation of France, Althusser was captured and placed in a German prison camp where he remained until the end of the war. Freed, he resumed his studies. In 1948, Althusser completed a master's thesis on the German philosopher Hegel, later passed the *agrégation* in philosophy and was given a teaching appointment.

Althusser was a practicing Catholic for the first thirty years of his life, and during that period displayed a strong interest in Catholic monastic life and traditions. In the late 1940s, Althusser joined the French Communist Party and remained a member for the remainder of his life. During the May 1968 Paris strikes, he was in a sanitarium recuperating from a bout of depression, an illness he struggled with throughout his life. Unlike some of his contemporary intellectuals, he supported the French Communist Party in denying the revolutionary nature of the student movement, though he later reversed this view.

Althusser murdered his wife in 1980. Declared incompetent to stand trial, he was institutionalized but released in 1983. He subsequently lived in near isolation in Paris and died in 1990 of a heart attack. During the last years of his life he wrote two different versions of his autobiography, both of which were published posthumously in 1992 (both are included in the 1995 edition of *The Future Lasts Forever*).

Althusser is especially important for the ways in which he reinterpreted Marx's ideas and made them resonate with intellectual currents prevalent in the 1960s, including structuralist ideas. Althusser's work is sometimes referred to as "structuralist Marxism" or "postmodern Marxism." Regardless of labels, his rereading of Marx aimed at liberating Marxist ideas from their Soviet interpretation, as well as from humanistic interpretations. This rereading was meant to revitalize Marxist ideas and to put them back to use for revolutionary purposes.

Of Althusser's many writings, three have been particularly influential: *For Marx* (published in French in 1965), *Reading Capital* (published in French in 1968), and the oft-cited long essay "Ideology and Ideological State Apparatuses" (written in 1969; included in *"Lenin and Philosophy" and Other Essays*). Althusser's influence has been widespread, shaping such diverse fields as cultural studies, film studies, and Marxist literary theory, though he has not been taken up to the same degree in performance studies.

Althusser's reassessment of Marxism included his rejection of some key Marxist assumptions about society. For instance, he argued against the version of determinism found in the classic Marxist formulation of **base and superstructure**. Base refers to the particular economic "mode of production" operating in a given society. Different societies are organized around different economic systems (modes of production) – for instance, agricultural, capitalist, or planned. The concept of superstructure refers to political, social, religious, and other non-economic aspects of a society. Superstructure, then, includes the political and cultural aspects a society, for instance, governmental, educational, religious, and other institutional structures. The traditional Marxist view was that base determines superstructure. That is, political, social, and cultural spheres – the superstructure – are not autonomous but are dependent on and conditioned by the economic mode, or base. Althusser prefers to talk about the idea of social formation (that is, society) consisting of three practices, the economic, the political, and the ideological. Althusser sees base and superstructure in relationship and affords superstructure considerable autonomy, though in the end, he concedes, the economic is determinant even if it is not dominant in a particular historical moment.

The term **practices** has a specific meaning for Althusser, indicating processes of transformation: "By *practice* in general I shall mean any process of *transformation* of determinate given raw material into a determinate *product*, a transformation effected by a determinate human labour, using determinate means (of 'production')" (*For Marx*, p. 166; emphases in original). Economic practices are concerned with using human labor and other modes of production in order to transform raw materials (nature) into finished (social) products. Political practices deal with the uses of revolution to transform social relations, and ideological practices concern the uses of ideology to transform lived social relations, that is, the ways a subject relates to the lived conditions of existence. Theory is often treated as the opposite of practice, but for Althusser theory is a type of practice.

The term **ideology** is central to Althusser's theoretical agenda. In "Ideology and Ideological State Apparatuses," Althusser melds ideas taken from both Marxist and psychoanalytic thought in order to develop his theory of ideology and its relationship to subjectivity. Althusser's central concern in this essay is with the question of how a capitalist society reproduces existing modes of production and their relationship to people. Why do people support this process when, according to Marxist thought, they are in effect acceding to their own domination by the ruling classes? Althusser formulates his answer through the concepts of ideology, ideological state apparatuses, and interpellation (on which see below).

The reproduction of capitalist society occurs at two levels, the repressive and the ideological. On the one hand, social control can be coerced by the exertion of repressive force through such institutions as police, armies, courts, and prisons – what Althusser calls **Repressive State Apparatuses** (RSAs). These institutions suppress dissent and maintain the social order as envisioned by the ruling power. But application of repressive force is not the only way to guarantee assent to capitalism. In addition to RSAs, Althusser argues that ideology must also be employed to maintain the dominant social formation. Althusser refers to these ideological modes of control as **Ideological State Apparatuses** (ISAs) – including education, family, religion, sports, television, newspapers, and other media – which reproduce capitalist values, standards, and assumptions. Ideological discourse produced by ISAs acts on individual subjects in such a way that they see themselves and others as standing within the dominant ideology, subject to it, and willingly supportive – consciously or unconsciously – of the replication of this ruling power. In short, ideology imposes itself on us, but at the same time we act, in effect, as willing agents of the ideological agenda.

Departing from the earlier Marxist notion that ideology is false consciousness, Althusser understands ideology as an inevitable aspect of all societies – even socialist societies where capitalist exploitation has presumably been destroyed – that serves, in part, to provide human subjects with identities. For Althusser, "Ideology represents the imaginary relationship of individuals to their real conditions of existence" ("Ideology and Ideological State Apparatuses," p. 162). Distinguishing between the imaginary and the real allows Althusser to counter the traditional Marxist notion that ideologies are false because they mask an otherwise accessible and transparent real world. In contrast to this notion of ideology as misrepresentation or false consciousness, Althusser views ideology as a narrative or story we tell ourselves in order to understand our relationship to modes of production. A real, objective world is not accessible to us, only representations of it.

Ideology, then, is a discourse that has marked effects on each individual subject. Althusser understands this effect through the concept of **interpellation**. Ideology hails and positions ("interpellates") individual subjects – or to state it another way, gives us a subject position – within particular discourses. As Althusser puts it, "ideology 'acts' or 'functions' in such a way that it ... 'transforms' the individuals into subjects" ("Ideology and Ideological State Apparatuses," p. 174). We assume our interpellated position, identify with received social meanings, locate ourselves within these meanings, and enact its goals under the guise of having freedom to make this choice in the first place. Althusser's structuralist notion of ideology is anti-humanist because it questions the centrality of the autonomous, freely choosing individual in this process. On the contrary, the subject is subjected to the ruling ideology, mistaking ideological interpellation for the actions of a freely choosing individual. It is noteworthy that Althusser uses a theatrical metaphor to describe the insertion of the subject into ideology. He compares the working of social reproduction to

> the mode of the stage direction (mise en scène) of the theatre which is simultaneously its own stage, its own script, its own actors, the theatre whose spectators can, on occasion, be spectators only because they are first of all forced to be its actors, caught by the constraints of a script and parts whose authors they cannot be, since it is in essence *an author-less theatre.*
>
> (*Reading Capital*, p. 193; emphasis in original)

Althusser provides an example of interpellation in action. Suppose, he says, an individual is hailed (interpellated) in the street by a policeman who says "Hey, you there!" The individual turns around to face the policeman. Althusser states, "By this mere one-hundred-and-eighty-degree physical conversion, he becomes a *subject*. Why? Because he has recognized that the hail was 'really' addressed to him, and that 'it was *really him* who was hailed' (and not someone else)" ("Ideology and Ideological State Apparatuses," p. 174; emphases in original). As this example suggests, interpellation is a performative process in which the individual becomes a subject by responding to the social prompts through which ideology works – in this respect, Althusser's understanding of ideology resembles other analyses of how subject formation occurs through performance, including those of Pierre BOURDIEU, Judith BUTLER, and Erving Goffman. Without necessarily knowing it, this subject is acceding to the ideology of state authority, its laws, and the systems that support and generate it. Ideology transforms us into subjects that think and behave in socially acceptable ways.

Although ideology is understood to subject individuals to the needs and interests of the ruling classes, it is not, according to Althusser, fixed and unchangeable. Rather, ideology always contains contradictions and logical inconsistencies, which are discoverable. This means that the interpellated subject has at least some room to undo or destabilize the ideological process. Change or revolution is possible.

Althusser explicitly addressed the politics of performance in one essay, "The 'Piccolo Teatro': Bertolazzi and Brecht. Notes on a Materialist Theatre," his commentary on a 1962 production by the Italian director

Giorgio Strehler whose work he saw as in tune with the principles of the German playwright and director Bertolt Brecht's materialist theatre practice (in *For Marx*, pp. 129–51). Mohammad Kowsar, in his reading of "The 'Piccolo Teatro'," points out that it is in Althusser's realignment of the traditional Marxist analysis of base and superstructure that one can glimpse how the possibility of social critique remains open for the interpellated subject:

> A theatrical performance, as a species of artistic activity (relegated to the field of ideology in Marxist thought – hence, the superstructure) cannot presume to effect absolute change. But superstructural activity, including theatrical practice and political philosophy, can very well demonstrate the conditions of change and act as a vanguard in the instigation of efforts toward transformation. Althusser consistently argues for a greater determinative role of the superstructure in the organizing principle between it and the structure or base.
>
> ("Althusser on Theatre," p. 469)

Kowsar further suggests that Althusser considered the critical potential of a materialist theatre to reside not in the ability of the performance itself to reveal contradictions and offer solutions but in the interaction between performance and audience:

> The spectator "participates with the actors, director and playwright, in the common condition of partial consciousness." This is why Althusser asserts "The play itself *is* the spectator's consciousness" (*For Marx*, p. 150); spectator and performance share by analogy the same limited knowledge that is straining to materialize into dialectical consciousness. . . . From the clash of two illusory consciousnesses (spectator versus performance) critically oriented toward replenishing what each lacks . . . a new ideological condition is born – whereby artistic activity justifies itself by participating in epistemological inquiry, and vice-versa.
>
> ("Althusser on Theatre," pp. 472–73; emphasis in original)

Timothy Murray uses Althusser's "The 'Piccolo Teatro'" essay to frame his defense of the political value of performances by such post-avant-gardists as Richard Foreman and Mabou Mines. Arguing that the return to frontal presentation in this work does not constitute a retreat to convention, Murray proposes that it refers to cinema, and that these performances carry out the mission of epistemological inquiry by providing their "viewers with the naked perception of the material structures on which they have been nurtured and by which they have been dominated" ("The Theatricality of the Vanguard," p. 98). However, Herbert Blau, reading the same essay, is not as sanguine as Murray concerning the ability of Althusser's formulation of a materialist theatre to provide spectators with such a direct view of the ideological apparatus. Detecting an undercurrent of pessimism in Althusser's otherwise reassuring assertion of the possibility of a socially critical performance practice, Blau observes that when Althusser says

> "the play itself is the spectator's consciousness" . . . there is still the problem, among the measures to be taken, of taking the measure of what is mostly made of fiction. . . . [W]hat unites the spectator to the play in advance does not necessarily guarantee an awakened criticism or a perception of the process by which the unity is engaged
>
> (Blay, *The Audience*, p. 278)

and may well end up simply reflecting and, thus, reifying those unifying ideological assumptions rather than creating the conditions for challenging them.

Further reading

By Althusser

For Marx. Translated by Ben Brewster. New York: Pantheon, 1969.

The Future Lasts Forever: A Memoir. Translated by Olivier Corpet, Yann Moulier Boutang, and Richard Veasey. New York: The New Press, 1995.

*"Ideology and Ideological State Apparatuses." In *"Lenin and Philosophy" and Other Essays*. Translated by Ben Brewster. London: New Left Books, 1971.

(with Etienne Balibar) *Reading Capital*. Translated by Ben Brewster. London: New Left Books, 1970.

About Althusser

Blau, Herbert. *The Audience*. Baltimore, MD: Johns Hopkins University Press, 1990.

Kaplan, E. Ann, and Sprinkler, Michael (eds). *The Althusserian Legacy*. London: Verso, 1993.

*Kowsar, Mohammad. "Althusser on Theatre." *Theatre Journal* 35, no. 4 (1983): 461–74.

*Montag, Warren. *Louis Althusser*. New York: Palgrave, 2003.

Murray, Timothy. "The Theatricality of the Van-Guard: Ideology and Contemporary American Theatre." *Performing Arts Journal* 8, no. 3 (1984): 93–99.

Payne, Michael. *Reading Knowledge: An Introduction to Barthes, Foucault, and Althusser*. Oxford: Blackwell, 1997.

Smith, Steven B. *Reading Althusser: An Essay on Structural Marxism*. Ithaca, NY: Cornell University Press, 1984.

Statkiewicz, Max. "Theatre and/of Ideology: The Notion of Spostamento in Althusser's Theory of Theatrical Praxis." *Rethinking Marxism* 10, no. 3 (1998): 38–50.

6   Mikhail Bakhtin

Key concepts

- theoretism
- everyday life
- unfinalizabilty
- dialogism
- heteroglossia
- dialogic truth
- carnival

Mikhail Mikhailovich Bakhtin (1895–1975) was a radical theorist of literature and language. Influenced by the writings of Karl MARX, he was particularly interested in social transformation and revolution within dominant
social and intellectual structures. Born in Orel, Russia, he was educated in
philology and classics at the University of Petrograd (1914–18), during the
time of World War I and the Russian Revolution. He taught in Nevel and
then Vitebsk, where he married Elena Aleksandrovna and became part of an
intellectual circle that also included Valentin Voloshinov and Pavel
Medvedev. He moved to Leningrad in 1924 and five years later was arrested
for alleged participation in the underground Russian Orthodox Church. On
account of ill health due to a bone disease, his initial sentence of ten years in
a Siberian labor camp was reduced to six years of internal exile in
Kazakhstan, where he worked as bookkeeper on a collective farm. After his
exile, he had no long-term stable employment until 1945, when he began
teaching Russian and world literature at Mordovia Pedagogical Institute
in Saransk, where he remained until his retirement in 1961. Indeed, his
academic life was so obscure that when scholars became interested in his
work in the 1950s (based mainly on *Problems of Dostoevsky's Poetics*, originally published in Russian in 1929), many were surprised to find that he
was still alive. In 1969 he moved to Moscow, where he remained until his
death in 1975.

In western Europe, initial interest in Bakhtin's work is owed primarily
to Julia KRISTEVA's famous 1969 essay, "Word, Dialogue, and Novel," in

which she engages his theory of dialogism (on which see below) in order to develop her theory of intertextuality. Kristeva also wrote the introduction to the French translation of *Problems of Dostoevsky's Poetics*, published in 1970.

Bakhtin worked on many topics over a half century of writing, from ethics to aesthetics. In all his work, however, there is a general concern with the relationship between ethical responsibility and creativity. Or to put it another way, he was interested in the relation between system and change, fixation and flux, law and revolution. How is change, as creative transformation of what is established and taken for granted, possible? What are the tensions within society, and within the self, between the desire for normativity and stability on the one hand and innovation and openness on the other? What is one's ethical responsibility to maintain and support established social order on the one hand and to bring about social transformation on the other?

From his earliest writings, he attacked **theoretism**, that is, the reduction of human creativity to a theoretical system. Theoretism impoverishes the truth of human life by subordinating all the complexity and messiness of human subjectivity and social relations to a static intellectual system.

Resisting theoretism, Bakhtin attended to the particularities of everyday life. Such attention to the minutiae of the everyday undermines the scholarly impulse toward universal theories. By the same token, he was drawn not to the grand or catastrophic events of human history – wars, disasters, revolutions, inaugurations – but **everyday life**, the "prosaic" details of the lives of ordinary people, details that are in many ways most revealing of human society and how social transformation takes place in history.

Throughout his work, Bakhtin emphasized **unfinalizability**, that is, the impossibility of any final conclusion. Nothing in life has been finalized, and nothing in life can ever be finalized. As he writes in *Problems of Dostoevsky's Poetics*,

> Nothing conclusive has yet taken place in the world, the ultimate word of the world and about the world has not yet been spoken, the world is open and free, everything is still in the future and will always be in the future.
>
> (*Problems of Dostoevsky's Poetics*, p. 166)

Life is riddled with surpluses, remainders, loopholes, and anomalies which keep things unfinalizable and therefore always hold open the possibility of surprise, change, and revolution. In this respect unfinalizability might be understood as that which undermines theoretism.

Related to unfinalizability is Bakhtin's theory of dialogism and dialogical truth, initially discussed in *Problems of Dostoevsky's Poetics* (see also his essay from the same period on "The Problem of Content," reprinted in his *Art and Answerability*). Whereas his earlier work focuses on the formation of the subject as an unfinalizable complex of identities, desires, and voices, his theory of dialogism focuses on discourse and language. **Dialogism** conceives of all discourse, in literature and in speech, as dialogical, that is, an intersection of multiple voices. When someone speaks and writes, her words are not simply streaming forth from within herself as sole author and source. Rather, her discourse, like her identity, is essentially a merger of the many voices and languages that constitute her as a subject. Every subject is made up of multiple voices, past and present, being a space of dialogue. One's speech and writing comes from that dialogical space, a space of **heteroglossia** (multiple and different voices). It is this theory of dialogism that KRISTEVA used to develop her theory of intertexuality, which conceives of every text and every discourse as a dialogical space, an "intersection of textual surfaces" (Kristeva, "Word, Dialogue, and Novel," p. 65).

So too with regard to what Bakhtin describes as **dialogical truth**. He identifies two kinds of discourse about truth: monological and dialogical. As the word implies, monological truth is presented as a single voice. It is one with itself and allows for no contradiction, no counter-voice, like a declaration from the Pope or the President. It is presented as though it is the final word – impossible as that may be. Dialogical truth, on the other hand, is the "truth" that emerges in the midst of several unmerged voices. It is an undirected intersection of voices manifesting a "plurality of consciousnesses" that do not all join together in one monologic voice. It is unsystematizable, unfinalizable. The "truth" of dialogical truth is not some particular statement about what is true and what is false, but rather the particularity and uniqueness of the event itself. It is not the unity of a system but the unity of a dynamic event, a dialogue that involves struggle and contradiction.

In *Problems of Dostoevsky's Poetics*, Bakhtin focuses on dialogism in literature. Most literary presentations of dialogue, Bakhtin readily concedes, are really presenting not dialogism but a series of monologic voices. Nonetheless he insists on the power of novelistic literature to be truly dialogical (as in Dostoevsky), drawing in multiple voices without subordinating them to any one voice, creating a space of interplay in which the author's function is that of a ringmaster who deploys various voices without identifying fully with any of them and the reader becomes a participant who must negotiate among these voices. In these respects, Bakhtin's ideas somewhat resemble those of Roland BARTHES on "the death of the author" and the "readerly text."

Another Bakhtinian concept that has gained much attention from scholars in a wide range of disciplines is **carnival**, an idea discussed in *Rabelais and his World*. Although Bakhtin derived his concept of carnival from cultural performances of the late medieval and early Renaissance periods in Europe, carnival is not limited to specific events but serves as an image of the will of the people apart from any social or political structure. Carnivals are playful subversions of the established social and political order of things, which might otherwise appear fixed. Through common practices of masquerade, the burning of effigies, the desecration of sacred objects and spaces, and excessive indulgences of the body, carnivals loosen the hold of the dominant order, breaking free – though only for a time – from law, tradition, and all that enforces normative social behavior.

Bakhtin emphasizes the participatory, encompassing aspect of carnival:

> Carnival does not know footlights, in the same sense that it does not acknowledge any distinction between actors and spectators. Footlights would destroy a carnival, as the absence of footlights would destroy a theatrical performance. Carnival is not a spectacle seen by the people; they live in it and everyone participates because its very idea embraces all the people. While carnival lasts, there is no other life outside it.
>
> (*Rabelais and his World*, p. 7)

In Bakhtin's thinking about carnival time, as throughout his work, we recognize his insistent attention to those aspects of life and language that underscore unfinalizability, keeping people and societies open to creative transformation – something that may have seemed particularly important in Stalinist Russia.

Within the field of performance studies, Bakhtin's theories of carnival and dialogism have enjoyed considerable influence, to the degree that it is impossible to summarize all the different contexts in which they have appeared. What follows is a very partial indication of the uses to which performance scholars have put Bakhtin's ideas.

Because Bakhtin derived his idea of carnival from a form of cultural performance and applied it to a work of literature, scholars working in both areas have found it applicable. Commentators on the history of Renaissance theatre and dramatic literature, including Shakespeare's plays, were among the first in the performance field to draw on Bakhtin: Michael D. Bristol's *Carnival and Theater* and Ronald Knowles's *Shakespeare and Carnival* are examples. Scholars have also found elements of the Bakhtinian carnivalesque in stand-up comedy, political demonstrations, British punk rock, and music video, among other forms of cultural and aesthetic performance. In "Carnivalesque Comedians," Marla Dvorak points to Canadian comic monologist Sandra Shamas's use of profane imagery and references to base bodily functions as well as the ambivalence of the laughter she generates: since there is no distinction in carnival between performer and audience, "by mocking the Other, we mock ourselves." In "Theatricalizing Politics/ Politicizing Theatre," Silvija Jestrovic refers to this same absence of distinction to describe the breadth of participation she observed at political rallies, which also serve to question the dominant order (albeit usually in terms of a specific policy, which was not what Bakhtin had in mind). Peter Jones also alludes in "Anarchy in the UK" to the democratic, participatory spirit of carnival to describe the sense within the punk music scene of the 1970s that the performers and audiences came from the same community. Jones also describes punk fashions and performance practices as inverting established practices and creating a grotesque body. Finally, Laura Madeline Wiseman suggests in "Carnivalesque and Bifurcated Labels" that Madonna's ability as a performer to continuously "morph and change," thus destabilizing conventional roles, aligns her with the carnivalesque.

Marvin Carlson points out that Bakhtin did not have dramatic dialogue in mind when he formulated the concept of dialogism; in fact, he found the speeches of dramatic characters to be monological because everything that happens on stage maintains the unity of the depicted world ("Theater and Dialogism," p. 314). Noting that Bakhtin based his analysis largely on classical tragedy, Carlson goes on to argue that the dialogism Bakhtin found in the novel can also be discovered in a great many modern plays and that the multitude of voices necessarily involved in theatrical production constitutes heteroglossia. Jurij Murasov also departs from Bakhtin's treatment of dramatic dialogue but moves in a different direction by arguing that Bakhtin reconceptualized theatrical language in terms of corporeality as well as participation; he applies this concept of the "organic language body" in "The Body in the Sphere of Literacy." Bakhtin has also influenced scholars concerned with oral interpretation and storytelling as well as theatre and performance art. Linda M. Park-Fuller suggests in "Voices" that the heteroglossia Bakhtin locates in the novel can be exploited when literary texts are performed. Richard Bauman takes up a different dimension of dialogism in *A World of Others' Words*, a study of the performance of oral literature, in which he examines the "relationships by which speakers may align their texts to other texts" through reiterative performance (p. 5).

Bakhtin's interests encompassed a broad range of cultural texts and contexts, ranging from the literary to the popular cultural. His legacy is clearly visible in the remarkable variety of cultural and aesthetic forms to which performance scholars have applied his ideas.

Further reading

By Bakhtin

Art and Answerability: Early Philosophical Essays. Edited by Michael Holquist and Vadim Liapunov. Translated by Vadim Liapunov. Austin, TX: University of Texas Press, 1990.

*The Dialogic Imagination: Four Essays. Edited by Michael Holquist. Translated by Caryl Emerson and Michael Holquist. Austin, TX: University of Texas Press, 1981.

Problems of Dostoevsky's Poetics. Edited and translated by Caryl Emerson. Minneapolis, MN: University of Minnesota Press, 1984.

*Rabelais and his World. Translated by Helene Iswolsky. Cambridge, MA: MIT Press, 1968.

Speech Genres and Other Late Essays. Translated by Vern W. McGee. Edited by Caryl Emerson and Michael Holquist. Austin, TX: University of Texas Press, 1986.

About Bakhtin

Bauman, Richard. *A World of Others' Words: Cross-Cultural Perspectives on Intertextuality*. Malden, MA: Blackwell, 2004.

*Bristol, Michael D. *Carnival and Theater*. New York: Methuen, 1985.

*Carlson, Marvin. "Theater and Dialogism." In *Critical Theory and Performance*. Edited by Janelle G. Reinelt and Joseph R. Roach. Ann Arbor, MI: University of Michigan Press, 1992.

Clark, Katerina and Holquist, Michael. *Mikhail Bakhtin*. Cambridge, MA: Harvard University Press, 1984.

Dvorak, Marla. "Carnivalesque Comedians." *Studies in Canadian Literature / Etudes en littérature canadienne* 20, no. 2 (1995). Online, available at: www.lib.unb.ca / Texts / SCL

Jestrovic, Silvija. "Theatricalizing Politics / Politicizing Theatre." *Canadian Theatre Review* 103 (2000). Online, available at: www.utpjournals.com

*Jones, Peter. "Anarchy in the UK: '70s British Punk as Bakhtinian Carnival." *Studies in Popular Culture* 24, no. 3 (2002). Online, available at: www.pcasacas.org / SPC

*Knowles, Ronald (ed.). *Shakespeare and Carnival: After Bakhtin*. New York: Plagrave Macmillan, 1998.

Kristeva, Julia. "Word, Dialogue, and Novel." Translated by Alice Jardine, Thomas Gora, and Leon Rudiez. In *The Kristeva Reader*. Edited by Toril Moi. New York: Columbia University Press, 1986.

Morson, G.S. and Emerson, C. *Mikhail Bakhtin: Creation of a Prosiacs*. Stanford, CA: Stanford University Press, 1990.

*Murasov, Jurij. "The Body in the Sphere of Literacy: Bakhtin, Artaud and Post-Soviet Performance Art." *Artmargins* (2001). Online, available at: www.artmargins.com

Park-Fuller, Linda M. "Voices: Bakhtin's Heteroglossia and Polyphony, and the Performance of Narrative Literature." *Literature and Performance* 7, no. 1 (1986): 1–12.

Wiseman, Laura Madeline. "Carnivalesque and Bifurcated Labels: Writing the Tale." *Nebula* 2, no. 1 (2005): 86–96. Online, available at: www.nobleworld.biz

7   Roland Barthes

Key concepts

- intertextuality
- the death of the author
- work versus text (textuality)
- the grain of the voice

Roland Barthes (1915–80) was a French literary critic and cultural theorist. Born in Cherbourg, France, he studied French and classics at the Sorbonne in Paris. He was active in protests against fascism and wrote for leftist journals and magazines. During World War II he taught in Paris, having been exempted from military service because of tuberculosis. After the war he taught in Romania, but later returned to school at the University of Alexandria where he studied linguistics with A.J. Greimas. He returned to Paris in the 1950s and worked at the Centre national de la recherche scientifique (CNRS) as a lexicographer and later as a sociologist. During this time, he wrote theatre criticism for *Théâtre populaire* and emerged as a strong advocate of the German leftist playwright Bertolt Brecht and an equally strong critic of what he considered the bourgeois tendencies of contemporary French theatre. He stopped writing on theatre by the end of the 1950s. From 1960 until his death he taught at the École practique des hautes études. In 1976 he was elected to a chair in literary semiology at the Collège de France. Along with several others discussed in this book, he was a member of the 1960s group organized around the literary journal *Tel Quel*. Barthes died in 1980 from injuries suffered when he was struck by a van while walking in Paris.

Barthes's intellectual career can be divided into two main parts. The first consists of structuralist interpretations of both popular culture and literature. This work was particularly informed by semiotics (i.e. the study of symbol systems) and based on Saussure's theory of the linguistic sign as an arbitrary signifier whose meaning is determined in relation to and over against other signs within the system. His early work was not only influenced by but also innovative within the field of structuralist analysis. His

1957 work, *Mythologies*, for instance, made a semiotic study of popular culture and everyday life, including analyses of sign systems found in such cultural forms as advertisements, fashion, and film (see also his 1964 essay, "Introduction to the Structural Analysis of Narratives").

Beginning in the late 1960s, Barthes turned away from structuralist analysis toward poststructuralism and deconstruction (on which see DERRIDA). During this latter period, Barthes developed and expanded on ideas that have significant implications for reading texts, including performances.

Here I will focus on Barthes's theoretical work during this second part of his career, especially two key short essays: "The Death of the Author" (1968) and "From Work to Text" (1971). In these articles – commonly regarded as marking his poststructural turn – Barthes delineates ideas that have impacted the way we read particular literary texts but also the way we understand the nature of textuality and interpretation in general. These two articles question traditional, commonsense conceptions of the role of the author and the reader, and explore differences in meaning and significance of a "work" and a "text." In them Barthes provides a critique of what are often understood as "natural" ways of reading and the "normal" relationship that pertains between author, reader, and text.

"The Death of the Author" is Barthes's critique of traditional conceptions of the author, the literary work, and reading. In effect it is a critique of the realist notion of representation, which views language as unproblematically providing an accurate representation of reality. Barthes challenges the assumption that reality is more or less fixed, stable, and representable by language.

Barthes questions the modernist strategy of looking at an author's life and body of work in order to discern the meaning of a particular text. In this Barthes is also critiquing his own earlier work, as in *Mythologies*, which treated cultural forms primarily as distinct and isolated from the larger world. Against this tendency to locate the meaning of a text in the intentions of its author, Barthes argues that texts can only be understood in relation to other texts. This is the notion of **intertextuality**, a term originally coined by his student and colleague Julia KRISTEVA (see also BAKHTIN's concept of dialogism). For Barthes, as for Kristeva, every text is part of a larger field of texts that provides its context of meaning. Every text is in dialogue with other texts. Meaning, therefore, is derived not from authorial intention but from the network of relations between the reader, the text, and the larger conceptual networks suggested by that text. It is on this basis that he announces **the death of the author**, echoing NIETZSCHE's pronouncement of the death of God decades earlier: "The birth of the reader must be at the cost of the death of the Author" ("The Death of the Author," p. 148).

Barthes's declaration that the author is dead is not merely an obituary for the old way of understanding textual meaning. Rather, it has important ramifications for where we understand meaning to reside. Remarking on the traditional understanding of the role of the author in transmitting textual meaning, Barthes observes that

> The explanation of a work is always sought in the man or woman who produced it, as if it were always in the end, through the more or less transparent allegory of the fiction, the voice of a single person, the author "confiding" in us.
>
> ("The Death of the Author," p. 143)

With the death of the author, a text becomes untethered from its author such that the author can no longer be considered the transcendent source of meaning of a text and the authority for how a text must be interpreted. Contrary to conventional views, texts do not transmit a singular, fixed meaning knowable by knowing the author's life history, cultural context, or intentions.

Referring to the author to obtain textual meaning serves to legitimize one's interpretation. As long as the authority of the author holds hegemonic sway, no other interpretation can be allowed or considered. But with the author symbolically dead, interpretation can move beyond the limitations of an author-centered way of reading. Barthes argues that "[o]nce the Author is removed, the claim to decipher a text becomes quite futile. To give a text an Author is to impose a limit on that text, to furnish it with a final signified, to close the writing" ("The Death of the Author," p. 147).

The death of the author means the intertextualizing of the text and the rise of the reader as the interpreter. The reader now has a more important role to play in generating textual meaning because the reader is now free to interpret a text regardless of authorial intention. We, as readers, have no access to what Barthes calls the "writer's interiority." In other words, we cannot know with any certitude an author's intentions in order to locate and fix a singular textual meaning. The import of this is that it frees interpretation from the notion of a singular, authoritative meaning that has ideological and hegemonic implications. Textual interpretation shifts to the reader's interpretation of the meaning of the linguistic signs in the text. An example of this style of poststructuralist reading appears in Barthes's book-length analysis in *S/Z* of a Balzac short story.

Barthes argues that texts never convey a single meaning, but are subject to multiple meanings and interpretations. These different interpretations are not merely the result of different readers with different perspectives, but rather primarily the result of the unstable and shifting meanings of words themselves, as well as the presence of innumerable intertexts. Words are unstable because they have meaning only in relationship to other words, and because the linguistic sign is both arbitrary and differential. It is this inherent instability of language that gives rise to multiple and competing interpretations of what a text means. This view of the linguistic sign is at once an assault on traditional views of representation because it repudiates the idea of a one-to-one relationship between word (signifier) and some external, fixed meaning in the world (signified).

For Barthes, then, all texts are intertextual. That is, they are embedded in a larger system of interrelationships among multiple texts existing within a cultural context. These texts – whether fiction or non-fiction, scientific or religious, whatever textual genre – are a part of every other text and each text is "a multidimensional space in which a variety of writings, none of them original, blend and clash" and "a tissue of quotations drawn from the innumerable centres of culture" ("The Death of the Author," p. 146). Further, the multiplicity of intertextuality is located in the reader:

> Thus is revealed the total existence of writing: a text is made of multiple writings, drawn from many cultures and entering into mutual relations of dialogue, parody, contestation, but there is one place where this multiplicity is focused and that place is the reader, not, as was hitherto said, the author. The reader is the space on which all the quotations that make up a writing are inscribed without any of them being lost; a text's unity lies not in its origin but in its destination.
>
> ("The Death of the Author," p. 148)

In "From Work to Text" Barthes extends his poststructuralist, intertextual view of textuality by detailing the emergence of the contemporary **text** over against the classical **work**. Though he does not put it this way, we might say that, for Barthes, the death of the author is also the death of the work. Barthes explains the distinction between work and text by analogy to the difference between Newtonian to Einsteinian physics. The work is like Newtonian physics in that it assumes a world that can be accurately and objectively represented. The text, on the other hand, is like Einsteinian science with its "demands that *the relativity of the frames of reference* be included in the object studied" ("From Work to Text," p. 156; emphasis in original).

The concept of the work can be understood as a counterpart of the living author. It reflects the traditional view of writing as the product of an individual who imbues the work with meaning. The work is a stable and contained entity that can be understood through knowledge of authorial intention and historical context. The work is also unproblematically representational. That is, its words point toward an external reality. It has a center that conveys a singular, stable truth; its meaning can be contained and controlled. The work is bounded – a thing that can be held in one's hands.

Unlike the work, the meaning of a text is unstable because it is subject to the play of meanings generated by the nature of language and intertextuality. The text is made up of what Barthes termed "a tissue of quotations drawn from the innumerable centres of culture" ("The Death of the Author," p. 170). It is this understanding of a text that readers engage with in order to wrestle with its many possible interpretations. If the work is a tangible thing that can be placed on a shelf, the text is to be understood rather as something indeterminate, unfixable; it is less a thing than a process of reading and interpretation. A text is multiple, contradictory, ambiguous, and its meaning uncontrollable. It has no center, just writing that generates more writing. It defers closure on a fixed truth or meaning. Note that in "From Work to Text," Barthes writes the term "text" with an uppercase "T" – Text – presumably to denote not a particular text but the concept of "text" or "textuality" more generally.

Timothy Scheie argues in "Performing Degree Zero" that even though Barthes was interested in the theatre during the early part of his career he did not produce a true theory of performance because he found it discomfiting that the live body could not be easily assimilated to the structuralist analysis to which he was intellectually committed. Nevertheless, Barthes can be said to have contributed to performance theory when writing about another art form, music. In his famous essay, **"The Grain of the Voice"** (1977), Barthes argues that one can hear aspects of some musical performances as produced directly by the performer's body and therefore as transcending cultural and textual norms. Grahame F. Thompson, in "Approaches to 'Performance'," places Barthes in one of four paradigmatic categories of performance theory. For Thompson, Barthes exemplifies those theories that view performance as the means by which the "outlines" contained in texts such as songs are filled in and supplemented by performance. "In the case of Barthes, it is actually the 'spilling out' over the outline that is the particular form of the problem" (Thompson, "Approaches to 'Performance'," p. 139).

Barthes anticipated some of the central concerns of performance studies. His analyses of professional wrestling, strip-tease, and chorus lines in *Mythologies* presage the expansion of the performance paradigm from the arts into the cultural field generally that is a hallmark of performance studies. Barthes also often self-consciously inserted himself into his writings, particularly in the final phase of his career – *Roland Barthes by Roland Barthes* (1977) is an important instance. In this respect, Barthes's critical practice anticipated the turn to "performative writing" in performance studies.

Barthes's theories of textuality and textual meaning have proved useful to students of contemporary performance practices. For example, his concept of the death of the author suggests that it is the audience that ultimately determines the meaning of a performance, not its creators, and that reception is therefore an important object of study. His insistence, along with KRISTEVA, that every text is fundamentally *intertextual*, a tissue of quotations drawn from innumerable other texts, cultural assumptions, and vested interests, is a valuable starting point for thinking about the work of experimental performance troupes such as the Wooster Group or the Builders' Association, who construct their texts on precisely those assumptions, as well as practitioners of devised performance, like Forced Entertainment, the authorship of whose texts, constructed through improvisation and experiment, is diffuse. It is equally applicable to more popular forms of performance and textuality, including turntablism, mash-ups, and the many other possibilities for cultural *bricolage* opened up by the advent of digital technologies.

Further reading

By Barthes

*"The Death of the Author." In *Image-Music-Text*. Translated by Stephen Heath. New York: Hill & Wang, 1977.

Elements of Semiology. Translated by Annette Lavers and Colin Smith. New York: Hill & Wang, 1968.

"From Work to Text." In *Image-Music-Text*. Translated by Stephen Heath. New York: Hill & Wang, 1977.

*"The Grain of the Voice." In *Image-Music-Text*. Translated by Stephen Heath. New York: Hill & Wang, 1977.

"Introduction to the Structural Analysis of Narratives." In *Image-Music-Text*. Translated by Stephen Heath. New York: Hill & Wang, 1977.

Mythologies. Translated by Annette Lavers. New York: Hill & Wang, 1973.

Roland Barthes by Roland Barthes. Translated by Richard Howard. New York: Hill & Wang, 1977.

S/Z. Translated by. Richard Miller. New York: Hill & Wang, 1974.

About Barthes

Auslander, Philip. "Toward a Concept of the Political in Postmodern Theatre." *Theatre Journal* 39 (1987): 20–34.

Culler, Jonathan. *Roland Barthes*. New York: Oxford University Press, 1983.

Lavers, Annette. *Roland Barthes: Structuralism and After*. Cambridge, MA: Harvard University Press, 1982.

Moriarty, Michael. *Roland Barthes*. Cambridge: Polity Press, 1991.

*Scheie, Timothy. "Performing Degree Zero: Barthes, Body, Theatre." *Theatre Journal* 52 (2000): 161–81.

Stafford, Andy. "Constructing a Radical Popular Theatre: Roland Barthes, Brecht and *Théâtre Populaire*." *French Cultural Studies* 7 (1996): 33–48.

Thompson, Grahame F. "Approaches to 'Performance': An Analysis of Terms." In *Performance: Critical Concepts*, Vol. I. Edited by Philip Auslander. London: Routledge, 2003. Originally published in *Screen* 26, no. 5 (1985): 78–90.

8 Georges Bataille

Key concepts

- communication
- heterology
- order of intimacy, order of things
- sacrifice
- search for lost intimacy
- festival

George Bataille (1897–1962) was born in Puy-de-Dôme, France. He converted to Catholicism in 1914, at age 17, though he lost his faith abruptly in 1920. He studied paleography and library science, and worked for 20 years at the Bibliothèque nationale. In 1951 he was named conservator at Bibliothèque municipale at Orléans. In a scholarly and artistic career spanning more than four decades, he wrote on a wide range of subjects, including numismatics, eroticism (he wrote erotic fiction as well as non-fiction on the subject of eroticism), autobiography, politics, literary criticism, philosophy, sociology, and religion.

Bataille was involved in a number of short-lived, radical anti-fascist groups, including the Surrealist movement (which denounced him in its Second Surrealist Manifesto in 1929) and the Democratic Communist Circle, which published the journal *La Critique sociale* (published from 1931 to 1934). He also organized a group called Contre-Attaque (1935–36) and soon after that helped found a "secret society" the public face of which was the now famous Collège de sociologie and its journal *Acéphale* ("headless") which ran from 1936 to 1939.

In all of his work, Bataille sought after human experiences that reveal the limits of thought, "other" experiences beyond representation in language – the burst of laughter, erotic love, potlatch, sacrifice, mystical union. He sought to highlight those experiences that exceed independent self-existence, experiences of disorientation and unknowing that shatter the self. Such experiences, Bataille believed, are what make **communication** possible, because they break open the self and put it into relation with others. The disintegration of the self is a kind of self-transcendence (transcending the self as a discreet body and mind), which opens one to the possibility of communion with others. In an early essay called "The Use-Value of D.A.F. de Sade (An Open Letter to my Current Comrades)" (written in 1929 or 1930), Bataille proposes a new academic program of study that focuses on this "other scene" of subversive excess, rupture, and self-transcendence. He calls this program **heterology**, defined as "the science of what is completely other" (*hetero* = "other") ("Use-Value," note 2). Indeed, heterology is an apt description of Bataille's entire life's work. Heterology attends to that which is other and therefore accursed within the dominant social order because it cannot be assimilated into it. It deals with that which is useless in a world driven by use-value and that which is wasteful in a world driven by production; it is what is pronounced evil in a world that reduces the sacred to moral goodness.

The "completely other" that is the focus of heterology is, for Bataille, closely related to notions of the "sacred" – but not as it is commonly associated in contemporary western discourse with goodness (versus evil) and reverence. Rather, he understands the sacred as fundamentally ambivalent: on the one hand, set apart as holy and revered; on the other hand, set apart as accursed and dirty. In a footnote, he writes that *agiology* – from the Greek *agio*, "holy" or "sacred" – might be a more appropriate term than heterology, "but one would have to catch the double meaning of *agio* (analogous to the double meaning of *sacer* [sacred]), *soiled* as well as *holy*" ("Use-Value," note 2).

Elsewhere in the essay he equates the "completely other" of heterology with the numinous, the wholly other, the unknowable, the sacramental, and the religious. He even considers whether his program should be called "religion" rather than "heterology," but is concerned that "religion" in modern western society is too closely associated with institutions that regulate and prohibit access to the sacred. For Bataille, religion was a field of activity and experience that could not be reduced to social utility or moral values. It does not simply make good workers and good citizens. There is within religion an impulse toward excess and extravagance that belies its orientation toward otherness and reveals its potential for subversion of social order.

In *Theory of Religion* (published in French in 1973, though written years earlier), which is closely related to his better-known three-volume *The Accursed Share*, Bataille conceives of two radically opposed regions or "worlds": the order of intimacy and the order of things.

The **order of intimacy** – also described by Bataille as the sacred world – is the realm of undivided continuity and flow in which there are no distinct objects or individual selves, an "opaque aggregate" (*Theory of Religion*, p. 36) reminiscent of the primordial chaos described in many creation mythologies. (This is also reminiscent of LACAN's pre-linguistic stage before individuation and subject formation, the Imaginary.) In intimacy there is no self-consciousness of oneself as an individual in relation to other individuals and objects. Bataille associates this realm with animality, for animals are "*in the world like water in water* . . . the animal, like the plant, has no autonomy in relation to the rest of the world" (p. 19; emphasis in original).

The **order of things**, which he also calls the profane or ordinary world, is the order of discontinuity, individuation, division and subdivision into subjects and objects. Whereas the order of intimacy is a realm of animality, the order of things is a realm of humanity. An early step out of the animal order of intimacy and into the human order of things was made when we began to use tools. A tool (a rock for hammering, a sharp stick for hunting) is something that we set apart and treat as an object, thereby positing ourselves as a subject. Thus the tool object and the tool-using subject are separated out of the undifferentiated continuity of intimacy and transformed into "things." We use the tool, moreover, to make and manipulate still other objects. In the process, we are self-objectifying, positing ourselves as an object in a world of other objects.

We experience this order of things, the "world of things and bodies," as the profane or ordinary world – "this world" over against a "holy and mythical world" of intimacy. The two worlds are incommensurable. "Nothing, as a matter of fact, is more closed to us than this animal life from which we are descended" (p. 20). So the order of intimacy, which is lost to us, is this world's wholly other, which is "vertiginously dangerous for that clear and profane world where mankind situates its privileged domain" (p. 36).

The privileged human domain of the order of things separates us from the order of intimacy and keeps it at bay – keeps it from breaking in and returning the order of things to primordial undifferentiated chaos.

> [Humankind] is afraid of the intimate order that is not reconcilable with the order of things. . . . [I]ntimacy, in the trembling of the individual, is holy, sacred, and suffused with anguish. . . . The sacred is that prodigious effervescence of life that, for the sake of duration, the order of things holds in check and that this holding changes into a breaking loose, that is, into violence. It constantly threatens to break the dikes, to confront productive activity with the precipitate and contagious movement of a purely glorious consumption.
>
> (*Theory of Religion*, pp. 52–53)

Bataille presents **sacrifice** as an exemplary expression of this **search for lost intimacy**. For Bataille, sacrifice is a failed effort at crossing over from the order of things to the intimate order. Rituals of sacrifice (*sacri-facere*, "to make sacred") take something with use-value within the order of things (a domestic animal, a person, a bushel of grain), removes it from that order, and passes it over to the order of intimacy – that is, to the realm of the sacred – through an act of wasteful consumption (burning, orgiastic feasting, etc.). Sacrifice is about wasting something that has use-value within the order of things, thereby sending it over to the other side, to the sacred realm of intimacy. This is why sacrificial animals are domestic rather than wild: a wild animal is already in the order of intimacy.

According to this idea of sacrifice, **festival**, carnival, and potlatch are also sacrificial practices. As John Lechte points out, potlatch for Bataille was not "a system of reciprocity" but, rather, part of a system of "expenditure without return" (Lechte, "Georges Bataille," p. 99). Such social practices are acts of sacred waste, removing valuables from the order of things by excessive (and therefore wasteful) consumption, and also, in the case of carnival, ruining social capital by mocking or otherwise subverting figures of public authority and law.

For Bataille, then, the violence of sacrifice must be distinguished from other kinds of violence, such as war. Contrary to patriotic proclamations that a soldier's death in battle is a sacrifice for a sacred cause (God, nation, capitalism), casualties of war are not sacrificial because they serve some cause deemed socially valuable. In war, the things and bodies that a people or nation expends are the price paid for advancing or maintaining some value within the order of things.

Although Bataille addressed many issues of interest to performance scholars, his work has had relatively little influence on performance studies. This is surprising in one way, since scholars affiliated with performance studies often characterize the field as a version of heterology: a discipline focused on the other, the local, and the marginal that operates at the interstices of other disciplines. Perhaps performance studies has neglected Bataille because the field has gravitated toward other theorists who deal with states that transcend or undo the normative and approach the sacred, in Bataille's sense (Mikhail BAKHTIN on carnival, Mihaly Csikszentmihalyi on the experience of flow, and Victor Turner on liminality and communitas, for instance).

Nevertheless, some commentators have found Bataille useful when dealing with forms of performance that focus on bodily excess and abjection, sacrificial violence, or anti-productive superfluity. In "After Us the Savage Goddess," Rebecca Schneider finds affinities between Bataille's interest in primitivism and the literal body as transgressive and the use of the "explicit body" in feminist performance art. Joanne Pearson, in "Time Wounds All Heels," has analyzed Isadora Duncan's emphasis of the bare female foot in dance in relation to Bataille's characterization of the foot as a part of the human body often disdained because of its perceived baseness. In "The Sacrificial Aesthetic," Dawn Perlmutter surveys a range of activities involving sacrificial violence and self-mutilation in performance art, body art, and various subcultures, using Bataille's discussions of the links between sacrifice, eroticism, and festival as points of reference. And in "Terminal Beach Party," Erik Davis describes the Burning Man Festival – an annual event in which a temporary community of artists is created in an uninhabitable part of the Nevada desert – as exemplifying the subversive commitment to anti-productivity that fascinated Bataille: "This was George Bataille's festival of excess, a potlach of useless gift-giving and random kindnesses."

Further reading

By Bataille

The Accursed Share, Volume 1: Consumption. Translated by Robert Hurley. New York: Zone, 1988.

The Accursed Share, Volume 2: The History of Eroticism; Volume 3: Sovereignty. Translated by Robert Hurley. New York: Zone, 1991.

"Autobiographical Note." In *The Bataille Reader.* Edited by Fred Botting and Scott Wilson. Oxford: Blackwell, 1997.

**The Bataille Reader.* Edited by Fred Botting and Scott Wilson. Oxford: Blackwell, 1997.

Erotism: Death and Sensuality. Translated by Mary Dalwood. San Francisco, CA: City Lights, 1986

Inner Experience. Translated by Leslie Anne Boldt. Albany, NY: State University of New York Press, 1988.

On Nietzsche. Translated by Bruce Boone. New York: Paragon, 1992.

Theory of Religion. Translated by Robert Hurley. New York: Zone, 1989.

"The Use-Value of D.A.F. de Sade (An Open Letter to my Current Comrades)." Translated by Allan Stoekl with Carl R. Lovitt and Donald M. Leslie, Jr. In *The Bataille Reader.* Edited by Fred Botting and Scott Wilson. Oxford: Blackwell, 1997.

About Bataille

Brown, Norman O. "Dionysus in 1990." In *Apocalypse and / or Metamorphosis.* Berkeley, CA: University of California Press, 1991.

Connor, Peter. *Georges Bataille and the Mysticism of Sin.* Baltimore, MD: Johns Hopkins University Press, 2000.

Davis, Erik. "Terminal Beach Party: The Burning Man, USA, 1995." *The Village Voice,* 31 October 1995. Online, available at: www.techgnosis.com

Gemerchak, Christopher M. *The Sunday of the Negative: Reading Bataille, Reading Hegel.* Albany, NY: State University of New York Press, 2003.

Hollier, Denis. *Against Architecture: The Writings of Georges Bataille.* Cambridge, MA: MIT Press, 1992.

Lechte, John. "Georges Bataille." In *Fifty Key Contemporary Thinkers.* London: Routledge, 1994.

*Pearson, Joanne. "Time Wounds All Heels: Duncan, Ballet, and Bataille." *Reconstruction* 3, no. 2 (2003). Online, available at: www.reconstruction.ws

*Perlmutter, Dawn. "The Sacrificial Aesthetic: Blood Rituals from Art to Murder." *Anthropoetics* 5, no. 2 (Fall 1999 / Winter 2000). Online, available at: www.anthropoetics.ucla.edu

*Schneider, Rebecca. "After Us the Savage Goddess: Feminist Performance Art of the Explicit Body Staged Uneasily across Modernist Dreamscapes." In *Performance and Cultural Politics.* Edited by Elin Diamond. London: Routledge, 1996.

Wernick, Andrew. "Bataille's Columbine: The Sacred Space of Hate." *CTheory.Net* (November 1999). Online, available at: www.ctheory.net

9   Jean Baudrillard

Key concepts

- simulation
- simulacrum
- postmodern
- hyperreality

Jean Baudrillard (1929–2007) was a postmodern cultural theorist who was particularly noted for his critiques of contemporary consumer society. Trained as a sociologist, he became one of the key theorists of postmodernity.

Baudrillard was born in Reims in northeastern France. His grandparents were peasant farmers and his parents worked in civil service jobs. At the University of Nanterre, he studied sociology under Henri LEFEBVRE. He taught sociology at Nanterre from 1966 until his retirement in 1987. His earliest work was written from the perspective of a Marxist sociologist, but in subsequent studies his intellectual mentors often came to be the objects of his critiques, including Lefebvre, MARX, and Sartre. Baudrillard's early engagement with Marxist theory was later abandoned after he embraced poststructuralist ideas in the 1970s. Baudrillard was also a student of the theories of Roland BARTHES and the mass media theorist Marshall McLuhan. Baudrillard's first book, *The System of Objects* (published in French in 1968), is a semiotic analysis of culture that was influenced by Barthes's poststructuralist ideas.

Baudrillard's work on postmodern culture – usually radical in its claims – utilizes ideas drawn from various disciplines including linguistics, philosophy, sociology, and political science. He addresses a wide range of issues, including mass media, mass consumption, consumer society, war, and terrorism. Baudrillard is best known for work, such as *Simulacra and Simulation* (published in French in 1981), in which he analyzes the nature of postmodern culture, asserting that contemporary culture can no longer distinguish image from reality. Baudrillard's view is that the "conventional universe of subject and object, of ends and means, of good and bad, does not correspond any more to the state of our world" (*Impossible Exchange*, p. 28).

Within the context of his explorations of postmodern western culture, Baudrillard is especially interested in representation. His work examines ways in which technology and media impact how we represent our experiences and what we can know about the world. Baudrillard argues that contemporary culture is so saturated with images from television, film, advertising, and other forms of mass media that differences between the real and the imagined, or truth and falsity, are indistinguishable. Images do not represent reality, but rather become reality. Our lives are thus **simulations** of reality in the sense that simulation constructs what counts as the real from conceptualizations that have no intrinsic or direct connection to reality. Images produced by mass media neither refer to reality nor harbor any independent meaning.

What are the implications of living in an image-saturated, postmodern society? In effect, our experiences of the world are mediated through the many images that confront us everyday and that frame how we see the world and what we see. Notions of the perfect body, for instance, come about not because of some unmediated experience we have in the world, but largely through all the body images projected by media, advertising, and other instruments of image production.

Central to Baudrillard's understanding of the relationship between reality and representations of it are the concepts of "simulacrum" and "hyperreality." A **simulacrum** is an image or representation of something. Baudrillard uses this term to refer to an image that has *replaced* the thing it supposedly represents. In "The Orders of Simulacra," Baudrillard distinguishes three phases, or "orders," of the simulacrum in western history. With each order, the image or simulacrum is increasingly alienated from that which it purports to represent. First order simulacra, which alter or mask reality, emerge prominently in the Baroque period, with its privileging of artifice over realism. Drawing from Walter BENJAMIN's essay, "The Work of Art in the Age of Mechanical Reproduction," Baudrillard identifies the emergence of second order simulacra with the modern age of mass production and its resulting proliferation of reproductions, that is, images of an "original" image, which in turn is an image of the "real" thing. It is an image of an image. Third order simulacra are the simulacra of the current **postmodern** age. In postmodernity, the simulacrum has lost all relation to reality. It is a production of reality, not an imitation. In postmodernity, the simulacrum has replaced the real so that we live in a world of simulacra.

Although images may appear to refer to or represent objects in the real world, "reflecting" a pre-existing reality, Baudrillard argues that in postmodernity images precede the real. If so, then we live in a world of simulation and not of reality. One characteristic of such a postmodern world is the proliferation of media for producing images that simulate reality, including photography, film, television, and the World Wide Web. Baudrillard says,

"To simulate is to feign to have what one doesn't have" (*Simulacra and Simulation*, p. 3). In short, simulation does not refer to reality or pretend to imitate it; rather, it constructs reality.

In *Simulacra and Simulation*, Baudrillard provides us with an example of how an image becomes reality itself. He cites a Borges story in which "the cartographers of the Empire draw up a map so detailed that it ends up covering the territory exactly" (*Simulacra and Simulation*, p. 1). The map, which is a representation of a real space, becomes the reality, or to use Baudrillard's term, a **hyperreality**: "Simulation is no longer that of a territory, a referential being, or a substance. It is the generation by models of a real without origin or reality: a hyperreal" (*Simulacra and Simulation*, p. 1). From this perspective:

> The territory no longer precedes the map, nor does it survive it. It is nevertheless the map that precedes the territory – *precession of simulacra* – that engenders the territory, and if one must return to the fable, today it is the territory whose shreds slowly rot across the extent of the map.
>
> (*Simulacra and Simulation*, p. 1)

For Baudrillard, the map has become the reality, not a representation of it. A hyperreal world, then, is one in which the real and the imaginary have imploded and the boundaries separating them no longer stand, nor do boundaries separating autonomous spheres. Thus, for instance, CNN and other cable news networks blur distinctions between fact, opinion, sports, politics, weather, and entertainment. The news does not describe or represent reality, it is reality. Baudrillard goes so far as to argue that media and other imaginary constructs function to create America itself as nothing more than a hyperreal simulation of the real. Overtly fictional environments like Disneyland serve to assure is that the rest of the country is real when it is, in fact, pure simulation.

Simulation commonly refers to something fake or counterfeit, unreal or inauthentic. But Baudrillard does not simply contrast simulation with the real; rather, he sees these as having suffered a radical disconnection. For Baudrillard, we can no longer meaningfully inquire about the relative truth or falsity of images and representations. Virtual worlds created by computer graphics underscore the idea that a reality can be created where there is no pre-existing reality that the virtual version represents.

Baudrillard draws on ideas related to performance in his discussions of simulation. In addition to Borges' map, one of Baudrillard's central images is that of someone simulating illness. This simulator is not organically ill but also is not just faking because the simulator "produces 'true' symptoms" of the illness (*Simulacra and Simulation*, p. 3) and there is no way of distinguishing "real" symptoms from simulated ones. In a related scenario, Baudrillard suggests testing reality by staging a hold-up as realistically as possible without its being real. "You won't be able to do it," he declares, the network of artificial signs will become inextricably mixed up with real elements (a policeman will really fire on sight; a client of the bank will faint and die of a heart attack; one will actually pay you the phony ransom).

(Simulacra and Simulation, p. 20)

Both of these examples are of performances that would not traditionally be considered ontologically "real" and yet are indistinguishable from the real. They serve as microcosms of the larger issues Baudrillard raises about a society given over to simulation. Arguably, the questions they raise have always been at the heart of theatre and other kinds of performance in which distinctions between reality and representation can become blurry and one can be taken for the other.

Elinor Fuchs points out that Baudrillard uses the theatre as an important trope in his discussion of the world's being overtaken by simulation: "he sees a world so intensely theatrical that theater has passed over into itself" and we can no longer distinguish the theatrical from the real (*The Death of Character*, p. 151). Baudrillard traces the evolution of this world back to the Renaissance. Associating "the great baroque theatrical machinery" with the production of "the false," he argues "theatre is the form which takes over social life . . . from the Renaissance on" ("The Orders of Simulacra," p. 87). One very pertinent question for performance studies is: What roles can performance assume in a hyper-theatricalized world given over entirely to spectacle and simulation? If one can no longer distinguish the theatrical from the real, what concepts of performance remain meaningful?

Baudrillard's writing has provided useful frameworks for performance theorists thinking about simulation as a mode of performance, especially in the context of digital or mediatized performance. For other theorists, the pertinent questions have to do with the situation of performance in a society dominated by mediatized representations and simulation, including issues surrounding the efficacy of political performance in that context.

Further reading

By Baudrillard

Impossible Exchange. Translated by Chris Turner. London: Verso, 2001.

Jean Baudrillard: Selected Writings, 2nd edn. Edited by Mark Poster. Stanford, CA: Stanford University Press, 2001.

*"The Orders of Simulacra." In *Simulations*. Translated by Philip Beitchman. New York: Semiotext(e), 1983.

Simulacra and Simulation. Translated by Sheila Faria Glaser. Ann Arbor, MI: University of Michigan Press, 1994.

The Transparency of Evil: Essays on Extreme Phenomena. Translated by James Benedict. London: Verso, 1993.

About Baudrillard

*Auslander, Philip. *Liveness: Performance in a Mediatized Culture*. London: Routledge, 1999.

Fuchs, Elinor. *The Death of Character*. Bloomington, IN: Indiana University Press, 1996.

Horrocks, Chris, and Jevtic, Zoran. *Introducing Baudrillard*. Lanham, MD: Totem, 1996.

Kellner, Douglas. *Jean Baudrillard: From Marxism to Postmodernism and Beyond*. Stanford, CA: Stanford University Press, 1989.

Kershaw, Baz. *The Radical in Performance: Between Brecht and Baudrillard*. London: 1999.

Kubiak, Anthony. "Disappearance as History: The Stages of Terror." In *Performance: Critical Concepts*, Vol. III. Edited by Philip Auslander. London: Routledge, 2003. Originally published in *Theatre Journal* 39 (1987): 78–88.

*Lane, Richard J. *Jean Baudrillard*. London: Routledge, 2000.

Murphie, Andrew. "Negotiating Presence: Performance and New Technologies." In *Performance: Critical Concepts*, Vol. IV. Edited by Philip Auslander. London: Routledge, 2003. Originally published in *Culture, Technology and Creativity*. Edited by Philip Hayward. London: John Libbey, *c.* 1990.

Schroeder, Franziska. "The Touching of the Touch – Performance as Itching and Scratching a Quasi-Incestuous Object." *Extensions: The Online Journal for Embodied Technology* 2 (2005). Online, available at: www.wac.ucla.edu/ extensionsjournal

Smith, M.W. *Reading Simulacra: Fatal Theories for Postmodernity*. Albany, NY: State University of New York Press, 2001.

Smith, Richard G. "Lights, Camera, Action: Baudrillard and the Performance of Representations." *International Journal of Baudrillard Studies* 2, no. 1 (2005). Online, available at: www.ubishops.ca/baudrillardstudies

10 Walter Benjamin

Key concepts

- the task of the translator
- the work of art in the age of mechanical reproduction
- aura
- exhibition value
- cult value

Walter Benjamin (1892–1940) was born in Berlin to a Jewish family which had largely assimilated to the city's Christian mainstream. He was educated at the universities of Berlin, Freiburg, Munich, and Bern. As a student he became involved in radical Jewish student movements and, along with his close friend Gershom Scholem, grew increasingly interested in Jewish mysticism. (Scholem went on to become a great scholar of Jewish mysticism.) In 1925 Benjamin submitted *The Origin of German Tragic Drama* as his *Habilitationsschrift* (a document required for promotion to a university position) at the University of Frankfurt. It was rejected because of its unconventional, lyrical style, and Benjamin never held a formal academic post. He worked as an independent scholar, freelance critic, and translator. Benjamin was friendly with the left-wing playwright Bertolt Brecht, with whom he corresponded and on whose work he commented frequently (his critical writings on Brecht were collected as *Understanding Brecht*, 2003). Benjamin's relationship with Brecht indicated a transition in his thinking during which his engagement with mysticism was tempered by an interest in Marxian historical materialism and cultural politics.

In 1933, with the rise of the Nazis in Germany, Benjamin moved to Paris, where he met Hannah Arendt among many other intellectuals. In 1939 he was deprived of his German nationality and spent time in an internment camp. In 1940, at the invitation of Theodor Adorno and Max Horkheimer of the School for Social Research (recently moved from Frankfurt to New York to escape the Nazis), Benjamin attempted to flee the French Vichy regime for the United States. When he arrived at Portbou on the Franco-Spanish border, he was refused entry into Spain. To return to France would have meant certain death. The next morning he was found dead, apparently a suicide by morphine overdose.

Benjamin wrote on a wide range of topics – from literary tragedy to modernity to Paris to messianism – and in a range of styles – from essay to commentary to aphorism. Artists, historians, literary critics and philosophers have all been drawn to his texts for their insight and provocation. Before turning to "The Work of Art in the Age of Mechanical Reproduction" (1936), Benjamin's most famous essay and arguably the one most directly connected with the concerns of performance studies, I would like to draw attention to the relevance of "The Task of the Translator" (1923) to performance.

In **"The Task of the Translator"** (an introduction to his translation of Baudelaire's *Tableaux Parisiens*), Benjamin examines the relation between an original literary work and its "afterlife" in translation. What is it that is being translated? With regard to any literary work worth translating, it is not simply information but "the unfathomable, the mysterious, the 'poetic,' something that a translator can reproduce only if he is also a poet" (p. 70). Translation is an art by which a literary work becomes something more than itself. In translation, the work has an "afterlife," which is something more than it was originally. Translation is a "stage of continued life." Therefore, in the work of the translator, the original work must die to itself in order to live beyond itself in another language as a work of literary art. At the same time, the original *calls for* its translation, because it in itself is incomplete and ultimately cannot reach the unfathomable mystery it seeks to attain. The task of the translator is not simply to convey the original's information to those who cannot read the original's language. Rather, it is a task of "recreation" aimed at liberating the poetic power of the text from its imprisonment within a particular (and necessarily non-universal, impure) language (p. 80). Benjamin's ideas on translation are clearly applicable to debates surrounding the relationship between text and performance in the performing arts, including theatre and music. Benjamin's argument that the original work is incomplete and calls for the translation of its poetic core into another language could be construed as supporting those who favor an open-ended approach to the process of moving from text to performance rather than literal stagings. As Patrick Primavesi suggests in "The Performance of Translation," Benjamin implies that translation is itself a kind of performance: translators restage the original text using literary gestures of their own choosing (p. 54).

Benjamin's now classic 1936 essay, **"The Work of Art in the Age of Mechanical Reproduction,"** explores the origins of the work of art in relation to what he believes to be a radically new era in art history brought on by new methods of mass reproduction. Important here is the concept of "authenticity," by which Benjamin refers to the original work of art's unique existence in time and space, "where it happens to be," in other words its "historical testimony" (p. 220). This is the essence or **aura** of the work of art that cannot be reproduced. It is what gives the original work its *distance*, its historical otherness in relation to us. Mechanical reproduction is driven by the desire to close that distance, "to get hold of an object at very close range by way of its likeness, its reproduction" (p. 223). And yet, with every reproduction, the aura of the original is diminished, because "the technique of reproduction detaches the reproduced object from the domain of tradition," alienating it from its original location, thereby substituting "a plurality of copies for a unique existence" (p. 221). Reproduction depends on that original work's aura (otherwise there would be no interest in reproducing it) even while it uproots it from the historical time and space that gives it its aura. Thus reproduction unwittingly liquidates the aura of the original work of art, substituting a simulation – a topic later explored by Jean BAUDRILLARD.

Benjamin further argues that the work of art's aura, its rootedness in tradition, has its basis in ritual. This, he insists, was the work of art's first and original use-value. Long before beauty or some other aesthetic experience was the artist's goal, and long before "art for art's sake," the work of art was made for use in religious ritual. Benjamin opposes **exhibition value to cult value**: as artists increasingly did their work with the explicit aim of public exhibition rather than ritual function, the work of art began to break free from its religious roots. Now, we are for the first time witnessing the radical "emancipation" of the work of art from "its parasitical dependence on ritual" (p. 224). In this new age, artists increasingly make their works with the conscious intention of reproducing them. The original is created for the purpose of its own reproduction. The work of art's reproducibility has become paramount, leading to a qualitative transformation of the nature of art.

One of Benjamin's central examples is the difference between stage acting and film acting: whereas stage performances are singular events, film acting is intended for reproduction. While the stage actor is fully present before his audience, the film actor performs directly for a machine (the camera) and only indirectly for an audience. Film actors are therefore unable to respond to their audiences and also have little control over their performances, which are ultimately shaped by directors and editors; in that sense, film actors are alienated from their own creative labor. Benjamin argues that in live stage performance, aura attaches not only to actors, but also to the characters they portray. On film, however, "the aura that envelops the actor vanishes, and with it the aura of the figure he portrays" (p. 229).

Like Brecht, Benjamin was interested in formulating the aesthetics of a leftist political art that would respond to changing social and technological conditions. He agreed with Brecht that this was not a question of imbuing artworks with a particular ideological content but of using techniques that would encourage the audience to adopt a socially critical attitude and that modern scientific developments provided a model for that attitude. Benjamin was struck by the testing procedures used in occupational psychology and believed that modern media, including radio and film, could be used in ways that would encourage a similarly analytical and objective perspective. In "The Work of Art in the Age of Mechanical Reproduction," he describes filmic techniques such as close-up and slow motion as enabling a new, deeper way of seeing reality that allows the spectator to perceive details that previously were invisible: "a different nature opens itself to the camera than opens to the naked eye" (p. 236).

Not only does film allow the audience to see things it previously could not, but also it encourages a critical attitude. Though the situation of the film actor may be one of alienation, that condition has a positive social dimension from Benjamin's point of view. The fact that the actor is not physically present before the audience

> permits the audience to take the position of a critic, without experiencing any personal contact with the actor. The audience's identification with the actor is really an identification with the camera. Consequently the audience takes the position of the camera; its approach is that of testing. This is not the approach to which cult values may be exposed.
> ("The Work of Art in the Age of Mechanical Reproduction,"
> pp. 228–29)

In a sense, the actor's loss is the audience's – and, therefore, society's – gain, since depriving actors of aura through technical mediation allows the audience to take a clear-eyed, critical view of the representations before them.

Benjamin did not argue that this critical perspective is inherent in the film medium; he notes that the entertainment industry uses the medium in the opposite way by replacing the actor's vanished aura with the "phony spell" of the movie star as commodity (p. 231). Even so, he finds film to be a revolutionary art form that has the potential to be used to advance social revolution.

Benjamin considers part of this potential to lie in film's status as a relatively democratic medium. Since film acting does not require traditional skill (because one can construct a performance on film simply by assembling shots) in principle anyone is as effective on film as anyone else. In that sense, film is potentially an inclusive, even interactive, medium. Benjamin uses a literary analogy, pointing out that whereas writing and publishing were once privileges reserved for the few, almost everyone now has the opportunity to publish: "today there is hardly a gainfully employed European who could not, in principle, find an opportunity to publish somewhere or other comments on his work, grievances, documentary reports, or that sort of thing" (p. 232). Similarly, "Any man today can lay claim to being filmed" (p. 231) and it is only because of the economic structure of the entertainment industry that people are deprived of that opportunity. Benjamin's notion that new technologies reshape people's ways of thinking and enhance their opportunities to communicate and be visible anticipates more recent phenomena, including home video, desktop publishing, the World Wide Web, and reality television. His corresponding caveat that while new media may encourage new forms of expression they do not necessarily serve a positive social or political function remains on point.

Although the shift from live media to film and broadcasting as dominant cultural forms that Benjamin perceived as new in the 1930s is by now simply a fact of life, his ruminations on what technological and perceptual change mean for art forms and their social functions continue to provoke valuable questions for students of performance. If Benjamin was right when he said that mechanical reproduction and exhibition value had routed the auratic, where does that leave live performance forms, which remain dependent on the perception of aura for their value and impact? Is it possible that we now perceive some technically mediated forms as auratic? What position does live performance occupy in a fully mediatized culture? Are some genres of performance better positioned within a cultural economy of mediatization than others? And what of the critical function of performance: what does it now take to encourage an audience to take up a socially critical stance?

Further reading

By Benjamin

The Correspondence of Walter Benjamin and Gershom Scholem, 1932–1940. Translated by Gary Smith and André Lefevere. New York: Schocken, 1989.

The Origin of German Tragic Drama. Translated by John Osborne. London: New Left Books, 1977.

* "The Task of the Translator." In *Illuminations.* Edited by Hannah Arendt. Translated by Harry Zohn. New York: Harcourt, Brace and World, 1968.

"Theses on the Philosophy of History." In *Illuminations.* Edited by Hannah Arendt. Translated by Harry Zohn. New York: Harcourt, Brace and World, 1968.

Understanding Brecht. Translated by Anna Bostock. London: Verso, 2003.

* "The Work of Art in the Age of Mechanical Reproduction." In *Illuminations.* Edited by Hannah Arendt. Translated by Harry Zohn. New York: Harcourt, Brace and World, 1968.

About Benjamin

Arendt, Hannah. "Introduction." In *Illuminations.* Edited by Hannah Arendt. Translated by Harry Zohn. New York: Harcourt, Brace and World, 1968.

*Auslander, Philip. "An Orchid in the Land of Technology: Walter Benjamin and Live Performance." In *Cultural Work: Understanding the Cultural Industries.* Edited by Andrew Beck. London: Routledge, 2003.

Bolz, Norbert and Van Reijen, Willem. *Walter Benjamin.* Translated by Laimdota Mazzarins. Atlantic Highlands, NJ: Humanities Press, 1996.

Doherty, Brigid. "Test and *Gestus* in Brecht and Benjamin." *Modern Language Notes* 115 (2000): 442–81.

Pontbriand, Chantal. "'The eye finds no fixed point on which to rest . . .'." Translated by C.R. Parsons. In *Performance: Critical Concepts*, Vol. IV. Edited by Philip

Auslander. London: Routledge, 2003. Originally published in *Modern Drama* 25 (1982): 154–62.

Primavesi, Patrick. "The Performance of Translation: Benjamin and Brecht on the Loss of Small Details." *TDR: Journal of Performance Studies* 43, no. 4 (1999): 53–59.

Zurbrugg, Nicholas. "Technology, Polypoetry and the Aura of Poly-performance." *Visible Language* 35 (2001). Online, available at: www.findarticles.com

11 Pierre Bourdieu

Key concepts

- habitus
- doxa
- cultural capital
- taste

Pierre Bourdieu (1930–2002) was a French sociologist whose work has been widely influential in both the social sciences and humanities. He was born in Denguin in rural southwestern France where his father was a postal worker. Bourdieu received a scholarship that enabled him to attend the prestigious Lycée Louis-le-Grand in Paris. He subsequently enrolled at the École normale supérieure, where he studied with Louis ALTHUSSER. After graduating with a degree in philosophy, Bourdieu taught first at high school level. In 1959 he was appointed to a position in philosophy at the Sorbonne, after which he taught at the University of Paris from 1960 to 1964. In 1964 he was named director of studies at the École des hautes études en sciences sociales and founded the Centre de sociologie de l'éducation et de la culture. In 1982 he was named chair of sociology at the Collège de France. He received the Médaille d'or (Gold Medal) from the Centre national de la recherche scientifique (CNRS) in 1993.

During his military service, Bourdieu spent time teaching in Algeria. This experience made him acutely aware of the social effects of French colonialism and the social inequality embedded in such a system. He later conducted ethnographic fieldwork in Algeria. This research was the foundation for many of his concepts and theories. Bourdieu also conducted fieldwork in France, where he studied the structures of social and class differences in French society. He was interested in how systems of social inequality are embedded in cultural practices. He paid particular attention to the study of the French education system and demonstrated how it reproduced class difference despite its claims to the contrary.

In 2001, Bourdieu became a celebrity with the appearance of a popular documentary film about him, *Sociology is a Combat Sport*. His books were often bestsellers in France. He matched his status as a public intellectual with political activism. Bourdieu was involved in fighting social injustice, publicly criticizing the inequalities in the French social class structure and supporting better conditions for, among others, the working classes and homeless people. He was also closely associated with anti-globalization movements.

Bourdieu's large body of work – he authored more than twenty-five volumes – covers a number of different areas, including the sociology of culture and taste, education, language, literature, and cultural aspects of museums. Among his best known texts are *Outline of a Theory of Practice* (published in French in 1972), *Distinction* (published in French in 1979), and *The Logic of Practice* (published in French in 1980). Many of his key concepts (e.g. habitus, doxa, and cultural capital) have had a significant and ongoing influence on the humanities and social sciences.

Blending structuralist perspectives on social systems with concern for individual human agency, Bourdieu seeks to understand patterns of human behavior and how they are generated by and within society. His concept of practice, developed in *Outline of a Theory of Practice*, figures significantly in how he explains the processes by which social patterns of behavior repro-duce structures of domination. By practice, Bourdieu refers to the things that people *do* as opposed to what they *say*. This is related to his concern with agency: how do individuals contribute to the reproduction of social restric-tions and what is it possible and not possible to do in a particular cultural context? Bourdieu develops the notion of practice through the concept of **habitus**. Bourdieu defines habitus as a system of

> durable, transposable *dispositions*, structured structures predisposed to function as structuring structures, that is, as principles of the generation and structuring of practices and representations which can be objec-tively "regulated" and "regular" without in any way being the product of obedience to rules.
>
> (*Outline of a Theory of Practice*, p. 72; emphasis in original)

In other words, a habitus is a set of dispositions that generate and structure human actions and behaviors. It shapes all practice and yet it is not experi-enced as repressive or enforcing. Its effects on us typically go unnoticed.

A specific habitus comes into focus when social and cultural markers such as occupation, income, education, religion, and taste preferences (food, clothing, music, and art) are juxtaposed one against another. For example, a corporate executive with an advanced college degree, disposable income, season tickets to the symphony, and a taste for fine wine contrasts with the dispositions (habitus) of a "blue collar" worker with a high school diploma and significant debt, who watches sports on TV, and prefers Budweiser to Bordeaux. Bourdieu locates habitus where these dispositions correlate as traits common to a particular social group or class. A specific set of such dispositions is what Bourdieu means by the term habitus.

Knowing the habitus of a particular person – what social group or class they fit into by virtue of a set of dispositions – does not provide the social scientist with predictive power to know what practices a person will engage in. To claim this would be to remove agency from individual actors, and valorize structure over practice. Bourdieu criticizes any method that would attempt to remove agency and practice from our understanding of social structure. Similarly, a habitus is not a fixed or static system. Bourdieu asserts that distinctions between one habitus and another are not rigidly set, but have a shared and processual quality. Dispositions are multiple – we may, for example, apply one set of dispositions in our home life and another while at work – and changeable over time.

How does one come to or learn a particular habitus? Bourdieu describes this process as one of informal, unconscious learning rather than formal instruction. One learns to inhabit a habitus through practical means, such as using a particular space for a specific purpose, listening to music, cooking, drinking, wearing clothes, driving cars, celebrating holidays, and giving gifts. The habitus one occupies shapes the practices that one engages in. For Bourdieu, the notion of habitus reveals that while a person's behavior may be in part determined by formal social rules and mental ideas – uncovered and described by the social scientist – a significant determinant of behavior is hidden, implicit knowledge learned informally and embodied in specific social practices. Once internalized, habitus dispositions are taken for granted. Bourdieu uses the term **doxa** to refer to the taken-for-granted, unquestioned, unexamined ideas about social life that seem commonsensical and natural to the one possessing these dispositions.

Bourdieu's notion of habitus is not simply about a process of socialization or enculturation into a set of practices, but is also concerned with the power relations that exist between social classes, that is, with how social inequality is perpetrated and maintained. Habitus functions to distinguish social classes from each other. It is Bourdieu's unique version of ideology. Habitus contrasts the different sets of dispositions (social expectations, lifestyle choices, etc.) that characterize different classes. Class distinctions appear clearly in the complex of practices embedded in a particular habitus. One reason why this is so socially powerful, according to Bourdieu, is because class inequalities and the dominance of one class over another occur covertly. Rather than the application of overt force, symbolic power is harnessed to maintain class distinctions and the appearance of their naturalness. Money may have economic exchange value for food and other commodities, but the possession and use of it also has symbolic exchange value that marks one as wealthy and upper class or poor and lower class. Domination occurs, in part, because the exchange value system is itself controlled by the dominant class.

In order to explain the relation between habitus and social stratification more fully, Bourdieu borrows the economic term capital, which he employs to refer not only to financial assets but also to other resources that confer status and reveal social class. Financial capital matters for the establishment of class distinctions, of course, but so does **cultural capital,** including educational level, linguistic competence, and other forms of capital that mark social class. Cultural capital is used to distinguish and maintain class distinctions and, by extension, social inequality. This is apparent in connections between different kinds of capitals: it is far easier to acquire the cultural capital of an elite university education if one possesses considerable economic capital than if one does not.

Bourdieu also employs the category of **taste** to describe how distinctions between high and low culture are made and justified. In his own research, he found correlations between French aesthetic preferences for the arts on the one hand and "taste" preferences for such things as food and fashion on the other. He found that such tastes, like other forms of cultural capital, serve to demarcate class differences. Because taste marks distinctions between different levels of socio-economic status and level of cultural refinement, it is also an ideological category. Thus, for Bourdieu, distinctions based on taste are part of the arsenal for differentiating social classes:

> Taste classifies, and it classifies the classifier. Social subjects, classified by their classifications, distinguish themselves by the distinctions they make, between the beautiful and the ugly, the distinguished and the vulgar, in which their position in the objective classification is expressed or betrayed.
>
> (*Distinction*, p. 6)

Given that Bourdieu includes taste in the performing arts as one of many aspects of habitus and indices of social standing, there is a natural connection between his work and theatre and performance studies. "Yet," as David Savran avers, "Bourdieu's name is virtually absent from work in either theater studies or performance studies" (Savran, "Choices Made and Unmade," p. 95). While this is true, it is also the case that some scholars in cognate fields have recognized connections between Bourdieu's notion of practice and the concepts of performance and performativity, and have employed his perspective in sociological examinations of performance. Anthropologist Rosalind Morris argues, for instance, that Bourdieu's theory of practice "actually helped to facilitate the current efflorescence of performativity theory in anthropology" because "it staged the discussion of ritual efficacy in terms that would resonate with Austinian – and hence [Judith] BUTLERIAN – notions of performativity, emphasizing forced and forceful reiteration rather than meaning" (Morris, "All Made Up," pp. 571–72). Britta Wheeler, a sociologist, uses Bourdieu as an important point of reference in theorizing the institutionalization of American performance art, a development that is distinctive for its paradoxical "development toward both popular entertainment and avant-garde art" (Wheeler, "The Institutionalization of an American Avant-Garde," p. 507).

Within theatre and performance studies, some thinkers have pointed toward Bourdieu as a source of methods for the kind of materialist, socio-logical analysis they feel is presently lacking in those fields. Maria Shevtsova sees in Bourdieu's concept of practice a heuristic for thinking about theatre as social practice: "Theatre practitioners as everyday individuals move . . . through the networks of social life, and the practice they do collectively – contact with spectators included – can neither be dissociated nor isolated from them" (Shevtsova, "Social Practice," p. 135). For his part, Savran offers a sketch of what a Bourdieuvian approach to the analysis of a theat-rical production that would attend to the embeddedness of performance practices within social practices might involve. It is worth quoting at length to provide a concrete indication of where the uptake of Bourdieu in theatre and performance studies might lead:

> How can one even begin to analyze Jonathan Larson's *Rent* and the per-formance of its celebrity without considering the constellations of ele-ments that comprise its habitus and its field? – the gentrification of the East Village; the commodification of queer and queer wanna-be culture; the mainstreaming of hip-hop; the prolonged economic boom that has particularly benefited the Broadway theater-going classes; the transub-stantiation of high into low, *La Bohème* into rock opera, as the occasion for slumming by members of these affluent classes; the romance of mis-cegenated cultural forms; the romance of miscegenation; the tragic mulatta updated as Latino drag queen in the wake of *Paris Is Burning*; the Disneyfication of Times Square, in relation to which the Nederlander Theater, gussied up to look dilapidated, becomes a theme park of abjec-tion; the intensifying pressure on nonprofit theaters to support them-selves by developing commercial fare for Broadway; the increasing obsolescence of the categories highbrow, middlebrow, and lowbrow; the trickle-up effect of MTV-style editing, graphics, and rhythms into almost every form of culture; the disappearance of bohemianism except as parody; the increasingly volatile relation in musical theater, especially after Stephen Sondheim, between economic capital and cultural capital; and finally, the sentimental mythologization of Larson's death on the eve of his immortality.
>
> (Savran, "Choices Made and Unmade," pp. 93–94)

Further reading

By Bourdieu

Distinction: A Social Critique of the Judgment of Taste. Translated by Richard Nice. Cambridge, MA: Harvard University Press, 1984.

The Field of Cultural Production: Essays on Art and Literature. Edited by Randal Johnson. Cambridge: Polity Press, 1993.

The Logic of Practice. Translated by Richard Nice. Stanford, CA: Stanford University Press, 1990.

Outline of a Theory of Practice. Translated by Richard Nice. Cambridge: Cambridge University Press, 1977.

About Bourdieu

Jenkins, Richard. *Pierre Bourdieu*, revised edn. London: Routledge, 2002.

Lane, Jeremy F. *Pierre Bourdieu: A Critical Introduction.* London: Pluto Press, 2000.

Morris, Rosalind. "All Made Up: Performance Theory and the New Anthropology of Sex and Gender." *Annual Review of Anthropology*, 24 (1995): 567–92.

Savran, David. "Choices Made and Unmade." *Theater* 31, no. 2 (2001): 89–95.

Shevtsova, Maria. "Social Practice, Interdisciplinary Perspective." *Theatre Research International* 26, no. 2 (2001): 129–36.

Shusterman, Richard (ed.). *Bourdieu: A Critical Reader.* Oxford: Blackwell, 1999.

Swartz, David. *Culture and Power: The Sociology of Pierre Bourdieu.* Chicago, IL: University of Chicago Press, 1997.

Wheeler, Britta B. "The Institutionalization of an American Avant-Garde: Performance Art as Democratic Culture, 1970–2000." *Sociological Perspectives* 46, no. 4 (2003): 491–512.

12 Judith Butler

Key concepts

* gender, sex
* performativity
* gender trouble
* paradox of subjection
* face of the enemy

Judith Butler (1956–) was born in Cleveland, Ohio, and is Maxine Elliot
Professor in the Departments of Rhetoric and Comparative Literature at the
University of California, Berkeley. She received her PhD in philosophy from
Yale University in 1984. Butler is best known as a theorist of gender, identity, and power. Her most influential book to date, *Gender Trouble* (1990),
makes the argument that neither **gender** nor **sex** are natural or given categories of human identity. At the time, this was a major challenge to the then-
common position among feminists that gender (masculinity and femininity)
is culturally constructed whereas sex (male and female) is natural and pre-
given. In *Gender Trouble* and the subsequent *Bodies That Matter* (1993),
Butler countered that

> gender must . . . designate the very apparatus of production whereby
> the sexes themselves are established. As a result, gender is not to culture
> as sex is to nature; gender is also the discursive / cultural means by
> which "sexed nature" or "a natural sex" is produced and established
> as . . . prior to culture, a politically neutral surface on which culture
> acts.
>
> *(Gender Trouble, p. 7)*

In other words, there is no male and female prior to cultural engenderings of
those two categories of identity. We cannot think outside our culture, and
"male" and "female" identities are as culturally determined as are "masculinity" and "femininity." That sexual identity is natural, that there are two
sexes in nature, is a cultural idea.

Butler argues that these categories of identity take social and symbolic form in a culture through repeated action. Sexual identity is **performative**. "There is no gender identity behind the expressions of gender; . . . identity is performatively constituted by the very 'expressions' that are said to be its results" (*Gender Trouble*, p. 25). Gender is not being but doing; it is not who you *are* but what you *do*, that is, how you express your identity in word, action, dress, and manner.

Butler is critical of forms of feminism that assert "women" as a group with a distinct identity, set of political interests, form of social agency, and so on. In making such assertions, she contends, feminism risks reinforcing a binary conception of gender, thereby reducing the infinite possibilities of social identity for human beings to two categories, man and woman, defined in opposition to one another. Against this, Butler calls for performances that produce **gender trouble** within this social and symbolic order: drawing out the contradictions and excesses within oneself – the parts that do not "come together" into a simple, unified "whole" self – and acting out a multiplicity of gendered and sexual identities. Thus a multiplicity of gendered and sexual identities would be produced, troubling the binary oppositions that reduce woman to man's other and vice versa, and opening up new forms of social agency and ways of being in the world.

In developing her theory of the performativity of gender and sex, Butler draws from both J.L. Austin's formulation of the linguistic performative and Michel FOUCAULT's understanding of power. Arguing against a reductionistic view of power as the dominant force of law, Foucault conceives of power as a "multiple and mobile field of force relations, wherein far-reaching, but never completely stable, effects of domination are produced" (Foucault, *The History of Sexuality, Volume 1: An Introduction*, p. 102). Power takes form within society through ceaseless struggles and renegotiations. It does not simply come down from on high but circulates through society. In the process it materializes, takes a "terminal form," within a particular socio-political system of power/knowledge. Yet the "terminal forms" that power takes are never entirely stable because they can never contain or totalize all actual and potential forces within it. Although they appear to us as terminal and fixed, they are in fact quite temporary and precarious. There are always points of resistance that cut across the social order and its stratifications of power and privilege, opening possibilities for subversion.

In *Gender Trouble* and later works, Butler develops Foucault's critical insights into the formation and subversion of terminal forms of power in relation to gender and sexual identity politics. Butler conceives of every social-symbolic order as a regulatory consolidation of power in the Foucauldian sense. Such an order is established and maintained by prohibitions and repeated performances of identities within that order. Yet, as Butler puts it, to be *constituted* within such a social-symbolic order is not to be *determined* by it. There is always the possibility of agency, of acting out within the system in ways that are subversive and transformative of it, because there are always aspects of oneself that are "socially impossible," that cannot be reduced to the order of things, that exceed any particular identity (such as gender identity and sexual identity) within that order. Hence her interest in drag, cross-dressing, and other queer forms of gender trouble. Butler calls for performances, that is, expressions of identity, that exploit those subversive dimensions and thereby produce new possible ways of being in society.

In *The Psychic Life of Power*, Butler engages FOUCAULT, FREUD, LACAN, ALTHUSSER, and others to explore a related paradox of social-symbolic agency, which she describes as the **paradox of subjection**. The paradox lies in the fact that subjectivity is founded on subjection. That is, in order to become an acting subject in a society, one must be subjected to its order (its language, laws, values, etc.). Recall Luce IRIGARAY's description of the social-symbolic order of patriarchy as "a certain game" in which a woman finds herself "signed up without having begun to play" (Irigaray, *Speculum of the Other Woman*, p. 22). So it is, in fact, with all forms of subjectivity. One acts *within* a certain social-symbolic order, a certain "game" with certain rules to which and by which she is initially "subjected." Even if her actions are ultimately subversive of that order, her subjectivity is inaugurated through subjection to it. Thus Butler writes: "Subjection signifies the process of becoming subordinated by power as well as the process of becoming a subject" (*Psychic Life*, p. 2). "A power exerted on a subject, subjection is nevertheless a power assumed by the subject, an assumption that constitutes the instrument of that subject's becoming" (*Psychic Life*, p. 11). To have power is, paradoxically, to be subjected to power. "What does it mean" she asks, "that the subject, defended by some as the presupposition of agency, is also understood to be an *effect* of subjection?" (*Psychic Life*, p. 11; emphasis in original). What it means, she argues, is that to be conditioned or formed by a certain terminal form of power is not to be determined by it. That is, a subject's agency, her own exercise of power, is not "tethered" to the conditions that formed her. The subject is, in one sense, an effect of power; through the same subject's own agency, power becomes the effect of the subject.

Butler has applied her theoretical interests in identity politics, subjectivity, and power to issues of ethics and violence in the war-torn aftermath of September 11, 2001. In particular, she focuses on media representations of the **face of the enemy**. How is it that America's enemies have been othered in such a way as to render them inhuman and their lives ungrievable, thereby turning us away from the reality of life as fragile and precarious? In exploring this problem in her essay "Precarious Life" (2003), Butler draws on Emmanuel LEVINAS's concept of the face-to-face encounter as an ultimate ethical situation, a moment of obligation to the other, who pleads "do not kill." Media images reduce the face of the other to enemy (both as target and as victim of war) and thereby rule out the possibility of a genuine face-to-face encounter in the Levinasian sense. In these media representations, the "ultimate situation" of the face-to-face is foreclosed. How, Butler asks, has the face of the other been erased by these dehumanized faces, and how does one tell the stories of these lives in such as way as to recuperate the ethical possibility of opening oneself to them in obligation and grief?

It is no exaggeration to say that Butler's influence on performance studies has been enormous, particularly through her work on the performativity of gender. That same work has also proved very controversial within the field, however, for several reasons. In Jon McKenzie's view, performance studies has adopted a paradoxical "liminal norm" from which emerges a characterization of performance as something that is inherently ambiguous and therefore always potentially subversive of the prevailing order. McKenzie credits Butler with having challenged this central premise of performance studies by creating "a theory of performativity not only as marginal, transgressive, or resistant, but also as a dominant and punitive form of power, one that both generates and constrains human subjects" (McKenzie, "Genre Trouble," p. 220). To many people in performance studies and other fields who are more used to the strong connections between theory and activism posited by feminist theory, among other kinds, this dual position seemed to result in political paralysis. Although Butler produced a compelling account of the way dominant regimes of power are sustained through the regular, performative reiteration of norms, she was much less forthright on how to produce social change. Her suggestion that subversive performances of non-normative identities could erode the dominant system over time left many unsatisfied (see the discussion of Slavoj ŽIŽEK's critique of Butler in this volume). Further, her rejection of identity politics, indeed of the traditional concept of identity itself, and of the idea that the physical presence of the body is foundational, also produced ripples of discomfort within performance studies, for which body and identity are central tropes.

The terms in which Butler differentiated performativity from performance were also perceived as problematic. In an oft-cited passage, Butler states:

> *performance as bounded "act" is distinguished from performativity insofar as the latter consists in a reiteration of norms which precede, constrain, and exceed the performer and in that sense cannot be taken as the fabrication of the performer's "will" or "choice;" further, what is "performed" works to conceal, if not disavow, what remains opaque, unconscious, un-performable. The reduction of performativity to performance would be a mistake.*
>
> ("Critically Queer," p. 24; italics in original)

To many in performance studies, Butler did not seem to allow the social performer much agency: power resides in the performativity of norms rather than in performances of identity. Elin Diamond, for one, critiques Butler's separation of performance and performativity by suggesting that Butler's concept of performativity is finally dependent on a concept of performance, because it is "only in the repetitive mutilations of performance . . . [that we can] gauge the power of performativity" (Diamond, "Re: Blau, Butler, Beckett," p. 36).

Despite these misgivings, both aspects of Butler's view of performance and performativity – the notion that power and social norms are performative and that particular performances can be subversive – have been taken up and used widely in performance studies. Performance scholars have extended Butler's initial focus on gender and sexual identity to other identity categories, including race (see Forbes) and disability (see Sandahl), and beyond the contemporary world to historical examples (see Franko). Butler can also be credited with having helped to communicate the performance studies perspective to other disciplines (presumably unintentionally); evidence of a "performative turn" in the work of cultural geographers (see Nash) and archivists (see Cook and Schwartz), among many others, shows how widespread her influence has been.

Further reading

By Butler

Bodies That Matter: On the Discursive Limits of "Sex." New York: Routledge, 1993.

"Critically Queer." *GLQ: A Journal of Lesbian and Gay Studies* 1, no. 1 (1993): 17–32.

* *Gender Trouble: Feminism and the Subversion of Identity.* New York: Routledge, 1990.

"Precarious Life." Meeting of the Consortium of Humanities Centers and Institutes, Harvard University, Cambridge, MA, March 15, 2003.

The Psychic Life of Power: Theories of Subjection. Stanford, CA: Stanford University Press, 1997.

About Butler

Case, Sue-Ellen. "The Emperor's New Clothes: The Naked Body and Theories of Performance." *SubStance* 31, nos. 2 and 3 (2002): 186–200.

Cook, Terry and Schwartz, Joan M. "Archives, Records, and Power: From (Postmodern) Theory to (Archival) Performance." *Archival Science* 2 (2002): 171–85.

Diamond, Elin. "Re: Blau, Butler, Beckett, and the Politics of Seeming." *The Drama Review* 44, no. 4 (2000): 31–43.

Forbes, Camille F. "Dancing with 'Racial Feet': Bert Williams and the Performance of Blackness." *Theatre Journal* 56 (2004): 603–25.

Franko, Mark. "Majestic Drag: Monarchical Performativity and the King's Body Theatrical." *The Drama Review* 47, no. 2 (2003): 71–87.

Jagger, Gill. *Judith Butler.* London: Routledge, 2006.

McKenzie, Jon. "Genre Trouble: (The) Butler Did It." In *The Ends of Performance.* Edited by Peggy Phelan and Jill Lane. New York: New York University Press, 1998.

Nash, Catherine. "Performativity in Practice: Some Recent Work in Cultural Geography." *Progress in Human Geography* 24, no. 4 (2000): 653–64.

Reinelt, Janelle. "Staging the Invisible: The Crisis of Visibility in Theatrical Representation." *Text and Performance Quarterly* 14, no. 2 (1994): 97–107.

Sandahl, Carrie. "Queering the Crip or Cripping the Queer? Intersections of Queer and Crip Identities in Solo Autobiographical Performance." *GLQ: A Journal of Lesbian and Gay Studies* 9, nos. 1–2 (2003): 25–56.

Walker, Julia A. "Why Performance? Why Now? Textuality and the Rearticulation of Human Presence." *Yale Journal of Criticism* 16, no. 1 (2003): 149–75.

13 Hélène Cixous

Key concepts

- Jewoman
- *écriture féminine*

Hélène Cixous (1937–) is Professor of Literature at the University of Paris VIII, an experimental university that she helped to found in 1968, and where she established a doctoral program in Women's Studies, the first and only one in France. Her childhood, as she describes it, was simultaneously Mediterranean and Nordic. Raised in Oran, Algeria, her father's Jewish family had fled Spain for Morocco and spoke French, Spanish, and Arabic. Her Jewish mother and grandmother were German, and German was spoken in her home. She also learned Arabic and Hebrew from her father before he died in 1948. She learned English as a student in London in 1950, and moved to France in 1955 where she became a student at Lycée Lakanal, a preparatory school for boys.

Given her life story, it comes as no surprise that she has always had a sense of homelessness and otherness wherever she found herself, without legitimate place, without "fatherland." Cixous captures this sense of home-lessness and hybridity in her self-description as "**Jewoman.**" "This is a thought, that we Jewomen have all the time, the thought of the good and bad luck, of chance, immigration, and exile" ("We Who are Free," p. 204). Indeed, for Cixous, this groundless multiplicity of selves – this experience of fitting in anywhere and nowhere, without fatherland and without singular identity – becomes, in writing, the source of creativity. Writing allows her to create a "country of words," a home away from home. It is precisely Cixous's sense of dislocation and perpetual immigration that, paradoxically, becomes the generative space of writing.

In an endorsement that has appeared on nearly every book by Cixous since the early 1990s, her longtime friend Jacques Derrida has called her the greatest contemporary writer in the French language. Part of what makes her writing so great, according to Derrida, is that she is a "poet-thinker, very much a poet and very much a thinking poet." Her writing is a kind of thinking about writing in which she follows her own creative process as it takes her into unfamiliar territories. "It's not a question of drawing the contours, *but what escapes the contour*, the secret movement, the breaking, the torment, the unexpected" ("Without End," p. 96; emphasis in original). It is precisely this self-reflective – often autobiographical – thinking about writing, as she encounters the "unexpected" while pursuing "what escapes," that has made her such an important figure for scholars concerned with theory. If she "does" theory, it is toward a theory of writing.

Indeed, we might think of Cixous's writing as a kind of *poetics of deconstruction*. As it follows what escapes the main contours of thought, she watches those contours dissolve and new landscapes emerge. In this process, she and her readers become increasingly aware that the main contours have been keeping them from unknown worlds of possibility. Writing thus becomes a process of opening toward the mystery of the other. "The prisons precede me. When I have escaped them, I discover them: when they have cracked and split open beneath my feet" ("We Who are Free," p. 203). In this respect she does with her poetic writing what her contemporary Julia KRISTEVA looks for in her early semiotic analysis of literature, that is, a kind of revolutionary poetic language which can produce an "other" kind of subjectivity capable of opening new possibilities for social relations and community that are subversive of the dominant patriarchal, capitalistic social-symbolic order.

A key concept in Cixous's early writings such as "The Laugh of the Medusa" (1975) and *The Newly Born Woman* (published in French in 1975), is that of *écriture féminine*, or feminine/female writing. Such writing has its source not just in poststructuralist Barthesian theory, but also in the embodied life experiences of women and is closely related to a woman's speaking voice. The author of this kind of writing "signifies . . . with her body." Contrasted against the univocal, authoritative, disembodied voice of the father identified with the symbolic order of things, *écriture féminine* is multivocal, "pregnant with beginnings," subversive, and embodied. In this kind of writing, moreover, there is a bond not only between the text and the body that wrote it, but also between that body and its original bond with the mother. In the lyrical voice of *écriture féminine* one may hear the mother's song, heard by the child before she could speak, that first voice which all women preserve in their own living voices.

In addition to being a novelist and theorist, Cixous is a playwright who, beginning in 1985, has collaborated frequently with director Ariane Mnouchkine and the Théâtre du soleil. In "Aller à la mer," a manifesto-like condemnation of the state of the theatre originally published in 1977, Cixous pointedly asks: "How, as women, can we go to the theatre without lending our complicity to the sadism directed against women, or being asked to assume, in the patriarchal family structure, that the theatre reproduces ad infinitum, the position of victim?" ("Aller à la mer," p. 546). Insisting that the theatre is a product of a masculine "narcissistic fantasy" that erases female subjectivity, Cixous calls for an approach to theatrical production that would be the equivalent of *écriture féminine*, a scenic practice rooted in the female "body-presence" that would eschew conventions of action, plot, and representation in favor of a form of expression based in the phenomenal experience of female corporeality. She cites her own play, *Portrait de Dora* (1976), a revisionist examination of one of Sigmund Freud's more problematic psychoanalytical case studies, as a first step that at least gave voice to the female subject.

Despite this strong stance, which was influential on feminist strains of performance theory, Cixous would describe her relationship to the theatre twenty years later by saying:

> as an author of fiction . . . I belong to no tradition, I am an explorer and I invent my territories. As an author of theatre, I feel that I belong in an uninterrupted manner to *the* tradition of theatre, the theatre of, from the origin, from the Greeks to Shakespeare. . . . I think that only in a tradition with a profoundly political message does the theatre have a reason for being. Particularly today, in quite an exceptional manner which distinguishes it from all other literary acts or practices, the theatre structurally carries a *responsibility in the instant.*
>
> (Fort, "Theater, History, Ethics," p. 428; emphases in original)

Cixous responds to this sense of urgency and responsibility by writing plays that deal with historical and contemporary political and social issues.

Further reading

By Cixous

* "Aller à la mer." Translated by Barbara Kerslake. *Modern Drama* 27, no. 4 (1984): 546–48.

"Coming to Writing" and Other Essays. Edited by Deborah Jenson. Translated by Sarah Cornell, Deborah Jenson, Ann Liddle, and Susan Sellers. Cambridge, MA: Harvard University Press, 1991.

* The Hélène Cixous Reader. Edited by Susan Sellers. New York: Routledge, 1994.

* "The Laugh of the Medusa." Translated by Keith Cohen and Paula Cohen from a revised version of "Le Rire de la Méduse." *Signs* 1 (1975): 875–93.

Rootprints: Memory and Life Writing. Edited by Hélène Cixous and Mireille Calle-Gruber. Translated by Eric Prenowitz. London: Routledge, 1997.

Three Steps on the Ladder of Writing. Translated by Sarah Cornell and Susan Sellers. New York: Columbia University Press, 1993.

"We Who are Free, are We Free?" Oxford Amnesty Lecture, February 1992. Translated by Chris Miller. *Critical Inquiry* 19 (1993): 201–19.

"Without End no State of Drawingness no, rather: The Executioner's Taking off." Translated by Catherine A.F. MacGillivray. *New Literary History* 24 (1993): 91–103.

(with Catherine Clément) The Newly Born Woman. Translated by Betsy Wing. Minnesota, MN: University of Minnesota Press, 1986.

About Cixous

Fort, Bernadette. "Theater, History, Ethics: An Interview with Hélène Cixous on *The Perjured City, or the Awakening of the Furies.*" *New Literary History* 28, no. 3 (1997): 425–56.

*Moi, Toril. *Sexual/Textual Politics: Feminist Literary Theory.* London: Routledge, 1985.

Scheie, Timothy. "Body Trouble: Corporeal 'Presence' and Performative Identity in Cixous's and Mnouchkine's *L'Indiade ou l'Inde de leurs rêves.*" *Theatre Journal* 46, no. 1 (1994): 31–44.

*Silverstein, Marc. "'Body-Presence': Cixous's Phenomenology of Theatre." *Theatre Journal* 43, no. 4 (1991): 507–16.

Willis, Sharon. "Hélène Cixous's *Portrait de Dora*: The Unseen and the Un-scene." *Theatre Journal* 37, no. 3 (1985): 287–301.

14 Gilles Deleuze and Félix Guattari

Key concepts

- rhizome
- aborescence
- becoming
- schizoanalysis
- desire as flow
- desiring machines
- body without organs
- deterritorialization

Gilles Deleuze (1925–95) was a philosopher. He was born in Paris and, after a long illness, committed suicide in 1995. He studied at the Sorbonne under Georges Canguilhem and Jean Hyppolite. He later taught philosophy at the Sorbonne, the University of Lyon, and, at the invitation of Michel FOUCAULT, at the experimental University of Paris VIII. He retired in 1987. Deleuze was a prolific writer, penning individual monographs on both philosophy and literature, including studies of Hume, Bergson, Spinoza, NIETZSCHE, Proust, Artaud, and Lewis Carroll, critiques of Kantian and Platonic thought, and considerations of such issues as representation, linguistic meaning, subjectivity, and difference.

Félix Guattari (1930–92) was a noted psychoanalyst and political activist. He was born in northern France and died of a heart attack in 1992. He embraced both radical psychotherapy ("anti-psychiatry") and Marxist politics, though he became disillusioned with the French Communist Party after the May 1968 Paris strikes. He was a psychoanalyst at the Clinique de la Borde from 1953 until his death, and was known for his use of alternative psychoanalytic therapies. Guattari was also closely associated with Lacanian psychoanalytic theory. He received training from Jacques LACAN and was in analysis with him from 1962 to 1969. He later came to critique at least some aspects of Lacanian analysis. Guattari individually published essays and two books on psychoanalytic theory. In addition to his work with Deleuze, he collaborated with other Marxist thinkers and psychoanalysts.

Deleuze and Guattari met in 1969 and started working together soon after. Their collaborations included four books that are especially noteworthy for their dual critiques of Marxist and Freudian thought. The writings I will deal with here are *Anti-Oedipus: Capitalism and Schizophrenia* (published in French in 1972) and *A Thousand Plateaus* (published in French in 1980). In these twin volumes, Deleuze and Guattari attempt to destabilize essentialism and grand theories – especially those of MARX, FREUD, and structuralism. Deleuze and Guattari leave us with a very rich conceptual palette replete with many neologisms, only a small part of which I can discuss here.

Despite the tendency among many to associate Deleuze and Guattari with "postmodernism," they did not themselves see their intellectual project in this light. Guattari, for instance, repudiated postmodernism as "nothing but the last gasp of modernism; nothing, that is, but a reaction to and, in a certain way, a mirror of the formalist abuses and reductions of modernism from which, in the end, it is no different" ("The Postmodern Impasse," p. 109). Their somewhat problematic relationship to postmodernism notwithstanding, Deleuze and Guattari crafted a view of the world critical of grand narratives (on which see the entry for LYOTARD), foundational thought, and essences. Resisting those tendencies of modern thought, their texts describe ways of seeing and understanding multiplicities both of individual subjects and larger institutional entities. It is to the end of destabilizing what they refer to as fascist ways of acting in the world that they arm themselves with a battery of neologisms that force us to think and conceptualize outside established, hegemonic, and naturalized modes of modern commonsense.

Through collaboration, and in keeping with their desire to understand subjectivity as multiple rather than singular, Deleuze and Guattari seek multiplicity in their writing style. As Ronald Bogue notes, their approach produces "a recognizable plural voice and thought irreducible to either writer's individual style or to a mere juxtaposition of the two" (Bogue, "Gilles Deleuze and Félix Guattari," p. 103). Any attempt to derive a clear and linear outline of their ideas runs counter to their own resistance to such modernist ways of thinking. Many of the neologisms they employ are more suggestive than definitive. But I can point out some of the recurring themes and concepts with which Deleuze and Guattari are concerned. In general, Deleuze and Guattari engage in insistent critiques of modern ideas concerning the primacy of hierarchy, truth, meaning, subjectivity, and representation. For instance, Deleuze and Guattari attack the notion that there exist individual subjects who can gain knowledge of the truth and then transmit (represent) that truth transparently to others.

One notion that underscores their attempt to derail modernist, linear thinking is their use of the metaphor of the **rhizome**, an idea taken up at the beginning of *A Thousand Plateaus*. A rhizome is a botanical term referring to a horizontal stem (like crabgrass), usually underground, that sends out roots and shoots from multiple nodes. It is not possible to locate a rhizome's source root. Rhizomatic thinking contrasts with **arborescent** (tree-like) thinking that develops from root to trunk to branch to leaf. Aborescent modes of thought, according to Deleuze and Guattari, are especially characteristic of the grand narratives of modernist, capitalist thought. Deleuze and Guattari protest:

> We're tired of trees. We should stop believing in trees, roots, and radicals. They've made us suffer too much. All of arborescent culture is founded on them, from biology to linguistics. Nothing is beautiful or loving or political aside from underground stems and aerial roots, adventitious growths and rhizomes.
>
> (*A Thousand Plateaus*, p. 15)

According to Deleuze and Guattari, the arborescent mode, which has dominated western thought, is hegemonic in that it naturalizes hierarchic orders and gives priority to narratives of origin. Rhizomatic thought suggests a non-hierarchy of multiple narratives without origin or central root to serve as the source.

To disrupt arborescent thought is to question modern conceptions of human subjectivity. Arborescence sees the world in terms of freely choosing, autonomous, individual entities – like free-standing trees. In such a mode of thinking, subject / object dichotomies abound. Deleuze and Guattari insist that we need to subvert this order through rhizomatic thinking that looks at the world in terms of relationship and heterogeneity. Deleuze and Guattari provide the example of the wasp and the orchid. Rather than describing each in the arborescent, hierarchical terminology of separate entities with distinct essences, Deleuze and Guattari require us to look at the interconnections, the points where the notion of individuality and essence break down. Thus, they state that "[w]asp and orchid, as heterogeneous elements, form a rhizome" (*A Thousand Plateaus*, p. 10). The point is this: from a rhizomatic perspective, the wasp and orchid are implicated with each other. The wasp is part of the orchid's reproductive process by transmitting pollen to it and the orchid provides food for the wasp. They form not a system of individual entities or nodes, but an interconnected, transitory, rhizome where the boundary of wasp and orchid are blurred. To understand this process we need to think not in terms of individual entities, but rather in terms of "a **becoming**-wasp of the orchid and a becoming-orchid of the wasp" (*A Thousand Plateaus*, p. 10).

The rhizome metaphor is a critique of totalizing processes, systems that attempt to explain all things within one interpretive framework or hierarchical master code. To this critical end, they mount a blistering critique of the Freudian and Marxist master narratives that ultimately limit the complexity of reality with their *transcendent* interpretations of human subjectivity and history. They oppose these dominant, transcendent modes of interpretation with an *immanent* mode of interpretation that acknowledges and prizes complexities. According to Deleuze and Guattari, fascist oppression is the inevitable result of transcendent interpretations.

The first volume of *Anti-Oedipus: Capitalism and Schizophrenia* takes up the political nature of desire. Deleuze and Guattari's criticism of psychoanalysis is made under the banner of **schizoanalysis**, a rhizomatic alternative to the arborescent thinking of psychoanalysis. In their schizoanalytic critique of Freud, Deleuze and Guattari refute Freud's negative notion of desire as lack that is explained through the Oedipus Complex. For Freud, the Oedipus Complex transcends time and place, and is a natural human disposition that is inescapable. For Deleuze and Guattari, this perspective is repressive because it subjects everyone to the same transcendent structure (mother – father – child). Rather than viewing the unconscious as characterized by desire and its lack, Deleuze and Guattari see the unconscious as productive of desire and hence in need of repressive control by the capitalist state. In analysis, the immanent interpretation of individuals is recast into the transcendent interpretation of Freudian desire, the family triangle. The individual is thereby subjected to the repression and restraint of the psychoanalytic interpretative framework, and the patient is subjected to the interpretation of the powerful and authoritative analyst.

Libidinal impulses are instead to be understood as *desire-producing* and therefore potentially disruptive of a capitalist state, which wants to control desire and cast it in negative terms. Similarly, culture, language, and other symbolic systems are also repressive because they subject people to their rules and codes. In contrast to the symbolic is the imaginary, and they refer to schizophrenia as exemplary of this mode. The Oedipal is symbolic; the pre-symbolic is pre-Oedipal and therefore prior to the hierarchy and repression of families (see also LACAN).

Schizoanalysis is a critique of psychoanalysis – an example of arborescent thinking – especially its conceptions of unconscious desire and the Oedipus Complex. In traditional psychoanalysis, which is a transcendent mode of interpreting human subjects, negative Oedipal desire precedes any particular patient's narrative. That is, the interpretation of the reported narrative is known in advance by the analyst. The outcome of analysis is predetermined. The only thing the analyst will find is Oedipal conflict. In turn, as a means of control, desire is directed toward oedipal prohibitions through this transcendent interpretation. "The law tells us: You will not marry your mother and you will not kill your father. And we docile subjects say to ourselves: so *that*'s what I wanted!" (*Anti-Oedipus*, p. 114; emphasis in original).

Deleuze and Guattari refer to schizophrenics as metaphorically exemplary of their arguments because of the fragmented nature of their subjectivity and desire that allows them to stand outside the repressions placed on the "normal":

But such a man produces himself as a free man, irresponsible, solitary, and joyous, finally able to say and do something simple in his own name, without asking permission; a desire lacking nothing, a flux that overcomes barriers and codes, a name that no longer designates any ego whatever. He has simply ceased being afraid of becoming mad. He experiences and lives himself as the sublime sickness that will no longer affect him.

(*Anti-Oedipus*, p. 131)

Desire, as conceived of in psychoanalysis, is something to be repressed and contained. Seeking to liberate desire from this negative charge, Deleuze and Guattari develop an understanding of **desire as a flow** of libido that exists prior to any representation of desire in psychoanalysis. Desire becomes "territorialized" through political and ideological structures like family, religion, school, medicine, nation, sports, and media. From an arborescent perspective, these structures subject the self – conceived of as autonomous – to their totalizing discourses. Deleuze and Guattari want to open possibilities for desire to flow in multiple ways and directions at once, regardless of socially sanctioned boundaries that otherwise seek to control that flow. Again, the schizophrenic stands for this possibility.

Deleuze and Guattari conceive of human beings as **desiring-machines**. This refers, in part, to the idea that desire stems from a moment prior to structure and representation. Bodies are desiring-machines, in which such things as ideas, feelings, and desires flow in and out of one body / machine and into and out of other desiring-machines. Desire is like a machine because it acts in ways very similar to a machine in that both are productive. For instance, a furnace-machine produces heat; desire produces libidinal energy. The idea of machine also subverts traditional views of subjectivity.

A desiring-machine is connected to a **body without organs** (often abbreviated BwO), a term borrowed from avant-garde playwright and theatre conceptualist Antonin Artaud (1896–1948). This concept denies the idea that the person is to be found inside the body, composed of autonomous, self-sustaining, and organized internal forms. Instead, it suggests the notion that the person / body is interconnected, exterior, open, multiple, fragmented, provisional, and interpenetrated by other entities. In their words:

There is no such thing as either man or nature now, only a process that produces the one within the other and couples the machines together. Producing-machines, desiring-machines everywhere, schizophrenic machines, all of species life: the self and the non-self, outside and inside, no longer have any meaning whatsoever.

(*Anti-Oedipus*, p. 2)

Schizoanalysis seeks **deterritorialization**, a space where desire is liberated from the constraints of the psychoanalytic. The deterritorialized is the space (both spatial and psychic) occupied by the metaphorical body without organs. This contrasts with territorialization and reterritorialization – the attempts to totalize, to structure hierarchically, to contain – through institutions such as religion, family, and school. To (re)territorialize is to try to contain and place boundaries around desire, to repress it. The deterritorialized is fragmented, multiple, uncontained. In such a space, boundaries are fluid, selves transform, desire flows in multiple directions.

Deleuze and Guattari emphasize decentered systems and uninhibited flows in their approach to the arts as well as in their critiques of psychoanalysis and political thinking. "The genuine work of art they see as decentered, nonunified, and subjective, immediately social, and engaged with the struggles of minorities in their various becomings – becoming-woman, becoming-black, becoming-child, becoming animal" (Bogue, "Gilles Deleuze and Felix Guattari," p. 103). For Deleuze and Guattari, *becoming* is a non-teleogical, continuous process through which any given entity may make rhizomatic connections to other things. As they explain it, a becoming is "neither one nor two, nor the relation of the two; it is the in-between" (*A Thousand Plateaus*, p. 293). One never finally becomes anything but is perpetually in a state of creative becoming.

Deleuze and Guattari's emphasis on becoming as an end in itself harmonizes with major trends in performance theory that likewise value action and process over result and product (performance itself is frequently defined in such terms). Deleuze and Guattari's aesthetic favors radical and innovative forms of performance: traditional acting, for example, in which the actor seeks to represent a fictional character, is arborescent inasmuch as the actor's portrayal is "rooted" in the presumptive reality of the text or character psychology. It is noteworthy that Deleuze's most sustained commentary on performance, entitled "Un manifeste de moins" ("One Less Manifesto") (1979) was inspired by the work of Carmelo Bene, an iconoclastic Italian actor and director whose productions frequently involved extreme dismantling of texts and radical discontinuities and incongruities (see Kowsar for a discussion of this text and Deleuze's collaboration with Bene).

Deleuze and Guattari's ideas have proved valuable as a critical framework for considering radically revisionist productions of classic texts (see Fortier) and the work of postmodern performance artists whose work not only is fragmentary and discontinuous but also may fall on the fault lines between forms – neither theatre nor dance, for instance, but some kind of rhizomatic theatre-becoming-dance (see Bottoms). Their analysis of decentered forms and systems has also proved pivotal for the analysis of performance that engages with digital technology, which permits the construction of precisely such branching systems (see e.g. Fenske). It is also significant, however, that Deleuze and Guattari's thought has proved inspirational not only to scholars studying performance but also to artists engaged in making performances, again presumably because of their emphasis on becoming. Their influence has been pervasive in the world of electronic music (see Ashline); there is even a German record label named Mille Plateaux (A

Thousand Plateaus)! In dance and theatre, Deleuze and Guattari's concept of becoming has served as a basis for workshop explorations of the performer's physical relationship to space and presence (see Claid) and the space between humanity and animal identity (see Chaudhuri and Enelow). Arguably, Deleuze and Guattari have had a greater direct impact on both the theory and practice of performance than any of the other theorists discussed in this volume.

Further reading

By Deleuze and Guattari

* *Anti-Oedipus: Capitalism and Schizophrenia.* Translated by Robert Hurley, Mark Seem, and Helen R. Lane. Minneapolis, MN: University of Minnesota Press, 1983.

* *A Thousand Plateaus: Capitalism and Schizophrenia.* Translated by Brian Massumi. Minneapolis, MN: University of Minnesota Press, 1987.

Deleuze, Gilles. "Un manifeste de moins." In Carmelo Bene and Gilles Deleuze, *Superpositions.* Paris: Minuit, 1979.

Guattari, Félix. "The Postmodern Impasse." In *The Guattari Reader.* Edited by Gary Genosko. Oxford: Blackwell, 1996.

About Deleuze and/or Guattari

Ashline, William L. "Clicky Aesthetics: Deleuze, Headphonics, and the Minimalist Assemblage of 'Aberrations.'" *Strategies: Journal of Theory, Culture and Politics* 15, no. 1 (2002): 87–101.

Bleeker, Maaike. "Sharing Technologies: Thought and Movement in Dancing." In *Micropolitics of Media Culture: Reading the Rhizomes of Deleuze and Guattari.* Edited by Patricia Pisters. Amsterdam: Amsterdam University Press, 2001.

* Bogue, Ronald. *Deleuze and Guattari.* London: Routledge, 1989.

Bogue, Ronald. "Gilles Deleuze and Felix Guattari." In *Postmodernism: The Key Figures.* Edited by Hans Bertens and Joseph Natoli. Belmont, MA: Blackwell, 2002.

Bottoms, Stephen J. "The Tangled Flora of Goat Island: Rhizome, Repetition, Reality." *Theatre Journal* 50, no. 4 (1998): 421–46.

Buchanan, Ian and Colebrook, Claire (eds). *Deleuze and Feminist Theory.* Edinburgh: Edinburgh University Press, 2000.

Chaudhuri, Una and Enelow, Shonni. "Animalizing Performance, Becoming-Theatre: Inside Zooësis with The Animal Project at NYU." *Theatre Topics* 16, no. 1 (2006): 1–17.

Claid, Emilyn. "Standing Still . . . Looking at You." *Research in Dance Education* 3, no. 1 (2002): 7–19.

Fensham, Rachel. "Beyond Corporeal Feminism: Thinking Performance at the End of the Twentieth Century." *Women: A Cultural Review* 16, no. 3 (2005): 284–304.

Fenske, Mindy. "The Movement of Interpretation: Conceptualizing Performative Encounters with Multimediated Performance." *Text and Performance Quarterly* 26, no. 2 (2006): 138–61.

Fortier, Mark. "Shakespeare as 'Minor Theater': Deleuze and Guattari and the Aims of Adaption." *Mosaic: A Journal for the Interdisciplinary Study of Literature* 29, no. 1 (1996): 1–18.

*Kowsar, Mohammad. "Deleuze on Theatre: A Case Study of Carmelo Bene's *Richard III*." *Theatre Journal* 38, no. 1 (1986): 19–33.

Massumi, Brian. *User's Guide to Capitalism and Schizophrenia: Deviations from Deleuze and Guattari*. Cambridge, MA: MIT Press, 1992.

Massumi, Brian (ed.). *A Shock to Thought: Expression after Deleuze and Guattari*. London: Routledge, 2002.

Stivale, Charles. *The Two-Fold Thought of Deleuze and Guattari: Intersections and Animations*. New York: Guilford Press, 1998.

15 Jacques Derrida

Key concepts

- deconstruction
- logocentrism
- presence
- supplementation

Jacques Derrida (1930–2004) was born into a petit-bourgeois Jewish family in the Algerian suburb El-Biar. At 10 years old, when the war came to Algeria, he and the other Jews were expelled from the public school system and then later (with the arrival of the allied forces) enrolled in a Jewish school. At 19 years old, he moved to France, where he began studies at the Grandes écoles preparatory program and studied phenomenology with Emmanuel LEVINAS. He taught at the École normale supérieure and the École des hautes études in Paris, and also held teaching posts at several American universities, including Johns Hopkins, New York University, and the University of California at Irvine. Throughout his career he demonstrated a strong commitment to public education, especially through his work with the Research Group on the Teaching of Philosophy, which advocates making philosophy a fundamental discipline in secondary school curriculum. He died of cancer in Paris in 2004.

It would be impossible to summarize Derrida's work, even if one were to limit oneself to his most influential contributions to philosophy, religion, linguistics, literary theory, and cultural studies. Yet there is a certain orientation that is consistent throughout his many texts. I might describe it as a kind of close reading that raises questions about "what is implicit in the accumulated reserve" (David, "An Interview with Derrida," p. 108). Through relentlessly vigilant attention to the texts and discourses in which the fundamentals of western thought are articulated, he worked to reveal the uncertainties, instabilities, and impasses implicit in our intellectual traditions, moving us to the edges of knowing, at which point "what once seemed assured is now revealed in its precariousness" (David, "An Interview with Derrida," p. 110). This was not, as his critics allege, out of some nihilistic contempt for all things western or masturbatory fascination with groundless intellectual free play, but in order to destabilize assumptions enough to open up spaces for continued reflection and the possibility of innovation and creative thinking. He treated western intellectual tradition as a living discourse and worked to keep our intellectual disciplines and educational institutions from ossifying.

This is the proper context in which to understand the term **deconstruction**, a concept that has too often been misunderstood by Derrida's readers, who do not always read him as well as he reads others. He first used it in *Of Grammatology* (published in French in 1967; translated and introduced in English by Gayatri SPIVAK) while trying to translate Heidegger's term *Destruktion*, which in French carried the sense of annihilation or demolition as well as destructuration. At the time "deconstruction" was used very little in French and its primary sense was mechanical, referring to the process of disassembly in order to understand parts in relation to the whole. For Derrida, deconstruction was conceived not as a negative operation aimed only at tearing down, but rather as a kind of close analysis that seeks "to understand how an 'ensemble' was constituted and to reconstruct it to this end" ("Letter to a Japanese Friend," p. 4). It is in the process of reading closely, with an eye for how an idea is constructed, that one also comes to see the points of potential rupture, the cracks and other points of instability within the structure. It is in the process of close reading that one sees deconstruction happening. "Deconstruction takes place, it is an event that does not await the deliberation, consciousness or organization. . . . It deconstructs itself" ("Letter to a Japanese Friend," p. 5). That is, it *loses its construction*. Deconstruction happens. It is a matter of reading closely enough to see it happening within systems that we might otherwise assume to be stable – indeed, systems that we *depend* on being stable.

Deconstruction, then, is what happens when one works one's way through a certain logic of thinking in such a way as to reveal what that logic cannot admit, what it must exclude, the unthinkable, "the singularity that threatens generality . . . the anomalies that circulate within and open up the system" (Sherwood, "Derrida," p. 71). As one of Derrida's early translators put it, "the deconstructive reading does not point out the flaws or weaknesses or stupidities of an author, but the *necessity* with which what he *does* see is systematically related to what he does *not* see" (Johnson, "Translator's Introduction," *Dissemination*, p. xv; emphases in original).

Throughout his career, Derrida was criticized for writing texts that are too difficult for many readers to understand. He defended his texts against such criticisms by pointing out why they are so difficult – namely, because they are fundamentally concerned with questioning precisely those things we think we understand. "No one gets angry with a mathematician or with a doctor he doesn't understand at all, or with someone who speaks a foreign language, but when somebody touches your own language" (David, "An Interview with Derrida," p. 107).

Derrida first emerged as a major influence on philosophy and literary studies in 1967, with the simultaneous publication in French of three books: *Speech and Phenomena*, a treatise on Husserl's phenomenology; *Of Grammatology*, a critique of the way western theories of language and communication have privileged speech over writing; and *Writing and Difference*, a collection of essays (some written as early as 1959) offering close readings of major contemporary figures including SAUSSURE, Lévi-Strauss, LEVINAS, and BATAILLE. Five years later, in 1972, he published three more: *Dissemination*, also on writing, with close readings of Plato, Mallarmé, and Sollers; *Positions*, a collection of interviews with him; and *Margins of Philosophy*, a series of close readings of philosophical texts, written at the margins of philosophical thought and in the margins of the texts themselves.

A year before his first book blitz in 1967, Derrida gave a lecture at Johns Hopkins University entitled "Structure, Sign, and Play in the Discourse of the Human Sciences" (later published in *Writing and Difference*). More than any other, it is this essay that led to widespread association of him with "poststructuralism," a term invented not by Derrida but by American literary scholars who were appropriating his theories in their own research. A brief synopsis of this now classic essay provides a helpful way into Derrida's early thought, which remains highly influential to this day.

Derrida presents this essay in the aftermath of the intellectual revolution of structuralism, a linguistic turn in the history of western thought which he sees as a transformative moment, a destabilizing of inherited understandings about the trustworthy stability of language and meaning. He describes this complex transformation as the

> moment when language invaded the universal problematic, the moment when, in the absence of a center or origin, everything became discourse . . . that is to say, a system in which the central signified, the original transcendental signified, is never absolutely present outside a system of differences.
>
> ("Structure, Sign, and Play," p. 280)

Here he is referring to the linguistic turn of structuralism inaugurated by SAUSSURE. This absence of a structural center, foundation stone, or ordering principal ("God," "Being," or some other "transcendental signified") to language, which would guarantee meaning and coherence within its system of signification, "extends the domain and the play of signification infinitely" (p. 280). Derrida uses the term **logocentrism**, which he also calls "the metaphysics of **presence**," to describe the belief that meaning is ultimately grounded in a transcendental signified. Here Derrida is not simply undermining Saussurean structuralism in the name of an infinite and unstable play of meaning; rather he is calling attention to the radical implication of structuralism, namely that *there is nothing outside language* to control, limit, or direct the play of signification. Signs are not inherently stable, so neither is meaning. Ultimate "undecidability" pervades all language.

Derrida then considers what our options are in the wake of the crisis in meaning he has just described. He identifies two responses, two "interpretations of interpretation." On the one hand, there is a melancholic, remorseful nostalgia for origins, a longing for "archaic and natural innocence" which "seeks to decipher, dreams of deciphering a truth or an origin which escapes play . . . and which lives the necessity of interpretation as an exile" (p. 292). Derrida sees Lévi-Strauss's search for the foundational elements of myth as an example of this mode of interpretation (another example may be found in Mircea Eliade's interpretation of cosmic religion as set against the profane homogeneity of modern society). On the other hand, there is the exuberant affirmation of play in a world without center or ground or security, as exemplified by NIETZSCHE. Both are responses to the modern western experience of being ungrounded and dislocated. While one aches with nostalgia for that which is forever lost, the other gets lost in limitless, homeless play.

Derrida does not imagine that his articulation of the structuralist catastrophe itself is any great revelation; nor is his delineation of these two ways of responding to that catastrophe. In this essay, the real revelation – of some common ground in this new groundless situation – is yet to come. The catastrophic ungrounding of western thought opens the world, as we know it and as we assumed it has always been known, to something radically other, proclaiming itself coming but not yet come.

In the mid-1960s, Derrida published two essays on the French theatrical visionary and one-time Surrealist, Antonin Artaud ("La Parole soufflée" in 1965 and "The Theatre of Cruelty and the Closure of Representation" in 1966 – both are available in English in *Writing and Difference*). For Derrida, Artaud was a kind of tragic figure who sought but failed to escape the grip of western metaphysics by conceptualizing a theatre that would transcend language in favor of direct physical communication, undo the theatre's dependence on a god-like author, and eschew repetition (and, hence, representation) in favor of unique events. Derrida both admired Artaud's confrontation with western tradition and emphasized the impossibility of his project. In these writings, the theatre is both symptomatic and emblematic of the western tradition, hopelessly locked into logocentrism. Artaud permits us to glimpse an alternative but not to escape the confines of tradition.

Derrida's influence on theatre and performance studies was most pronounced in the mid-1980s and was closely related to his influence on literary criticism. The two primary issues on which his work was brought to bear in the context of performance were textuality and presence. In an essay of 1983 ("The Play of Misreading: Text/Theatre/Deconstruction") Gerald Rabkin proposes that deconstructive criticism – which follows Derrida's celebration of play by emphasizing that texts have no stable meanings and are open to creative "misreadings" – provides a new approach to thinking about the relationships among text, performance, and criticism in the theatre. He suggests that the habit of thinking of the play text as the logos or referent of the production, the function of which is to reveal meanings contained in the text, could be undone by deconstruction's revelation of the instability of all texts, and that deconstruction was also a valid trope for understanding what experimental directors did with texts. In a related vein, Elinor Fuchs, writing in 1985, pointed to the ways some contemporary playwrights and directors were exposing the textual underpinnings of their productions, thus deconstructing the ostensible immediacy of the spoken word in the theatre ("Presence and the Revenge of Writing: Rethinking Theatre after Derrida"). Taking up a different aspect of Derrida's analysis of textuality, Marvin Carlson proposed the Derridean concept of **supplementation** – the idea that no text is ever complete or stable because a supplementary text can always alter its meaning retrospectively, and every supplement can in turn be supplemented – as a model for the relationship between text and performance in theatre ("Theatrical Performance"). The performance history of a particular play thus becomes an endless chain of supplements, none more definitive than any other. In "Just Be Yourself: *Logocentrism* and *Différance* in Performance Theory," originally published in 1986, Philip Auslander examines the implications of the more purely philosophical aspects of Derrida for ideas about acting. Auslander argues that most twentieth-century theories of acting suppose that the actor's performance is grounded in a concept of the actor's self, understood logocentrically as the truth of that person. Auslander deconstructs the self/performance binary by demonstrating that in several of the major modern theories of acting, the "self" that supposedly grounds the performance is actually produced by the process of performing.

Further reading

By Derrida

Dissemination. Translated by Barbara Johnson. Chicago, IL: University of Chicago Press, 1981.

"Letter to a Japanese Friend." In *Derrida and Différance.* Edited by David Wood and Robert Bernasconi. Warwick, UK: Parousia Press, 1985.

Of Grammatology. Translated by Gayatri Spivak. Baltimore, MD: Johns Hopkins University Press, 1976; corrected edition, 1998.

Specters of Marx: The State of the Debt, the Work of Mourning and the New International. Translated by Peggy Kamuf. New York: Routledge, 1994.

*Writing and Difference. Translated by Alan Bass. Chicago, IL: University of Chicago Press, 1978.

About Derrida

Auslander, Philip. "Just Be your Self: *Logocentrism* and *Différance* in Performance Theory." In *From Acting to Performance: Essays in Modernism and Postmodernism.* London: Routledge, 1997.

Caputo, John D. *Deconstruction in a Nutshell: A Conversation with Jacques Derrida, with a Commentary by John D. Caputo*. New York: Fordham University Press, 1997.

Carlson, Marvin. "Theatrical Performance: Illustration, Translation, Fulfillment, or Supplement?" In *Performance: Critical Concepts*, Vol. II. Edited by Philip Auslander. London: Routledge, 2003. Originally published in *Theatre Journal* 37, no. 1 (1985): 5–11.

David, Catherine. "An Interview with Derrida." Translated by David Allison. In *Derrida and Difference*. Edited by David Wood and Robert Bernasconi. Warwick, UK: Parousia Press, 1985.

Fuchs, Elinor. "Presence and the Revenge of Writing: Rethinking Theatre after Derrida." In *Performance: Critical Concepts*, Vol. II. Edited by Philip Auslander. London: Routledge, 2003. Originally published in *Performing Arts Journal* 9, nos. 2–3 (1985): 163–73.

Rabkin, Gerald. "The Play of Misreading: Text/Theatre/Deconstruction." *Performing Arts Journal* 7, no. 1 (1983): 44–60.

Royle, Nicholas. *Jacques Derrida*. London: Routledge, 2003.

Sherwood, Yvonne. "Derrida." In *Handbook of Postmodern Biblical Interpretation*. Edited by A.K.M. Adam. St. Louis, MO: Chalice, 2000.

Thiher, Allen. "Jacques Derrida's Reading of Artaud: 'La Parole Soufflée' and 'La Cloture de la Representation'." *French Review* 57, no. 4 (1984): 503–08.

16 Michel Foucault

Key concepts

- archaeology of knowledge
- discourse
- genealogy
- power
- ethics of self

Michel Foucault (1926–84) was a French philosopher, social and intellectual historian, and cultural critic. He was born in Poitiers, the son of upper-middle-class parents. He went to Paris after World War II and was admitted to the esteemed École normale supérieure in 1946, where he received degrees in philosophy (1948), psychology (1949), and his *agrégation* in philosophy (1952). Like many other French intellectuals in the 1940s and 1950s, Foucault became a member of the French Communist Party in 1950, but he left the Party in 1953 after reading NIETZSCHE.

During the 1950s and early 1960s, Foucault held teaching positions at European universities while conducting research and writing his first widely influential books, including *Madness and Civilization* (published in French in 1961; submitted two years prior for his doctorate), *The Birth of the Clinic* (published in French in 1963), and *The Order of Things* (published in French in 1966), which became a bestseller in France and made Foucault a celebrity.

In response to the May 1968 strikes and student demonstrations, the French government opened the University of Paris VIII at Vincennes. Foucault, who had been working in Tunisia in May 1968, was named chair of its philosophy department. In 1970, Foucault was elected to the Collège de France, the country's most prestigious academic institution. This permanent appointment – as Professor of the History of Systems of Thought – provided Foucault with a position in which he could devote nearly all his time to research and writing. His only teaching-related responsibility was to give an annual sequence of a dozen or so public lectures on his work.

It is during this same period of time that Foucault became increasingly involved in social and political activism. His advocacy of prisoner rights, for example, influenced his history of the prison system, *Discipline and Punish* (published in French in 1975). Around the same time he turned his attention to sexuality, publishing the first of three volumes on the *History of Sexuality* in 1976. He completed the other two volumes shortly before his death from AIDS-related complications in 1984.

Regardless of how one evaluates Foucault's scholarship, there is little doubt that the questions and issues he raised have permanently reshaped the humanities and social sciences. Foucault's scholarly output is impressive both for its quantity and for its breadth of interests and ideas. Among the topics he examined are madness, punishment, medicine, and sexuality. Foucault's work relentlessly challenges what counts as commonsense knowledge about human nature, history, and the world, as well as the social and political implications of such knowledge. Along the way, he questions the assumptions of such modernist masters as FREUD and MARX whose ideas often underpin intellectual commonsense in twentieth-century France. More specifically, Foucault explores the parameters of what he calls the "human sciences," that academic field in which humanistic and social science discourses construct knowledge and subjectivity. He often writes on how various institutions (psychiatric clinics, prisons, schools, etc.) produce discourses that then constitute what can be known or practiced relative to that body of knowledge. People become disciplined subjects within these different discourses. In the process he shows how knowledge and power are intimately connected. Therefore terms such as discourse, subjectivity, knowledge, and power are key to understanding Foucault's theories. These concepts, in turn, can be positioned within three areas that were central to Foucault's cultural analysis: (1) archaeology of knowledge, (2) genealogy of power, and (3) ethics. Underlying all three areas is a concern with the notion of the "subject" and the process of subjectivization, that is, the process by which a human subject is constituted (see also Judith BUTLER on the paradox of subjection, which she develops in relation to Foucault).

The **archaeology of knowledge** is the name Foucault gives (in a book by that title first published in French in 1969) to his method of intellectual inquiry. For Foucault, archaeology refers to a historical analysis that seeks to uncover **discourses** operating within systems of meaning. His concern is not with uncovering historical "truth," but rather with understanding how discursive formations – for example, medical discourse or discourse on sexuality – come to be seen as natural and self-evident, accurately representing a world of knowledge. Influenced by structuralism, Foucault sought to uncover structures and rules embedded in discourse through which knowledge is constructed and implemented. Discursive knowledge regulates, inter alia, what can be said and done, what constitutes right and wrong, and what counts for knowledge in the first place. In short, discourse establishes and controls knowledge. Medical discourse thus establishes

medical knowledge and related practices, including the doctor–patient relationship, divisions between physical and mental illness, the value of medical
services, status hierarchies within the medical profession, and who can
produce medical discourse itself. Significantly, Foucault's archaeological
method regards discourses as both fluid and mutable, and systematic and
stable. Medical discourse during the Renaissance bears no necessary similarity to contemporary medical discourse, yet each has a distinctive historical archive. It is these historical shifts that Foucault aims to uncover
through the archaeology of knowledge. He examines discourses of madness,
reason, and mental asylums in *Madness and Civilization* and discourses of
medical practice and the medical "gaze" in *The Birth of the Clinic.*

During the 1970s Foucault devoted his research to what he described as
the genealogy of power, that is, a history of the meanings and effects of
power, and how discourse and "technologies of power" are employed to
discipline human behavior. The term **genealogy** is used by Foucault to refer
to a mode of historical analysis that that he developed in texts such as
Discipline and Punish (1975) and *The History of Sexuality, Volume 1: An
Introduction* (1976). The concept of genealogy, borrowed from Nietzsche, is
explained by Foucault in his 1971 article, "Nietzsche, Genealogy, History."

Foucault's understanding of the nature of history is significant for the
way in which it subverts the commonsense teleological view of history as a
narrative of the causes and effects that produce human events and are thus
traceable, in a linear and logically satisfying fashion, backwards to origins.
Foucault also sees history as narrative but one that is fragmented, non-
linear, discontinuous, and without the certitude of cause and effect. Foucault
refers to this form of historical analysis as genealogy and describes it thus:
"Genealogy is gray, meticulous and patiently documentary. It operates on a
field of tangled and confused parchments, on documents that have been
scratched over and recopied many times" ("Nietzsche, Genealogy, History,"
p. 139). For Foucault, history is textual and conveys a narrative that is
ambiguous and conflicting. History bears the marks of repeated emenda-
tions – additions, deletions, embellishments, and other textual tinkering that
makes it impossible to follow a cause and effect lineage back to an origin.
For Foucault, any origin has long become obscured and unrecoverable.
Historical truth suffers a similar fate, though truth claims are still made and
are difficult to controvert. Foucault, following Nietzsche, sees truth as error:
"Truth is undoubtedly the sort of error that cannot be refuted because it was
hardened into an unalterable form in the long baking process of history"
("Nietzsche, Genealogy, History," p. 144).

Genealogy as a method underscores the interpretive nature of any narra-
tion of the past (on which see also Hayden WHITE). Indeed, the historical
past is always and inevitably read through contemporary interests and
concerns. Objectivity is questioned in favor of acknowledging the historian's political and ideological investment in the narrative being told. Even if
historical truth exists, historians have no particular or privileged access to it.

Foucault is most interested, then, in understanding historical documents as discourses of knowledge that highlight some perspectives while suppressing others. Foucault wants to reread the past and narrate that story from other perspectives. This genealogical approach runs counter to an idea of history as relating the "truth" of past events – of telling what "actually" happened. Rather than chasing after some ephemeral grand narrative that attempts to silence the discontinuities, Foucault seeks to interpret the past in ways that highlight the ambiguity, fragmentation, and struggle that necessarily accompanies any historical analysis. For Foucault, if the concept of historical origin must be invoked then it also must be acknowledged that there are multiple origins for any historical trajectory. History as one unified story gives way to a multiplicity of narratives about the past. Thus, we begin to see history not in terms of a static and fixed past but as a continually changing narrative process.

Foucault applies his genealogical analysis to the history of **power**, exploring how power operates to produce particular kinds of subjects. For Foucault, power is not some monolithic force that appears in the same guises throughout all times and places. Instead, power has a genealogical history and is understood differently depending on place, location, and theoretical perspective. For instance, a Marxist view of power as that force wielded by governments, corporations, and others who control the economic means of production is very different from a feminist view of patriarchal power. Similarly, Foucault sees power as having a history that includes instances of both oppressive power and power as resistance to oppression. Foucault argues in "The Subject and Power" (1982) that the concept of power must always include the possibility of resistance to power. Power, therefore, is always a relationship, one that creates subjects. But power relationships can be resisted which means that we can oppose the subject positions that discourses and material practices attempt to impose on us. For Foucault, power is capillary, flowing throughout the social body and not simply emanating from on high.

Genealogical inquiry is used by Foucault to further explicate ways in which power is implicated in how subjects and subjectivity are constructed. As Foucault noted in a 1980 lecture at Dartmouth College,

> I have tried to get out from the philosophy of the subject through a genealogy of this subject, by studying the constitution of the subject across history which has led us up to the modern concept of the self. This has not always been an easy task, since most historians prefer a history of social processes, and most philosophers prefer a subject without history.
>
> ("About the Beginning of the Hermeneutics of the Self," p. 160)

A genealogical view of subjectivity is Foucault's way out of such essentializing views of the human subject as a singular, transcendent entity.

In his later work, Foucault takes up the issue of the **ethics of self**. But ethics of self does not simply mean an individual's "morals." Rather, he is interested in identifying "techniques" or "technologies" of the self, that is, the regularized forms of behavior that constitute a particular human subject. Such technologies, which include sexual, political, legal, educational, and religious patterns of behavior, may be taken for granted or even go completely unnoticed by the subject who is constituted by them. Nonetheless they function to *discipline* the body and mind within a larger order of power/knowledge. Techniques are subjectivizing practices that create and shape one's sense of self. These subjectivizing practices are not universal, but variable over time and place. By focusing on these technologies of the self, he aims to uncover how they are implicated in the construction of subjects.

For Foucault, technologies of the self are practices

> which permit individuals to effect by their own means, or with the help of others, a certain number of operations on their own bodies and souls, thoughts, conduct, and way of being, so as to transform themselves in order to attain a certain state of happiness, purity, wisdom, perfection, or immortality.
>
> ("Technologies of the Self," p. 146)

Significant here is the ethical idea that individuals can resist power and transform their own subjectivity by applying techniques of the self. While techniques of the self are about discipline, they are not simply about discipline as domination of the self; they also entail positive transformations of the self.

Foucault argues that morality has three references: (1) to a moral code, (2) to behaviors in relation to that code, and (3) to ways that a person conducts oneself. Foucault is primarily concerned with this last aspect. For him, self-conduct deals with how individuals view and create themselves as ethical subjects. This runs counter to notions of morality as measuring one's behavior against a transcendent moral code. In his three-volume study of sexuality, for instance, Foucault is interested in the question of how and why sexuality became an object of moral discourse as opposed to other areas – say, for example, food or exercise.

Many of Foucault's ideas have found a conceptual home in performance studies. In an essay of 1992 entitled "Waiting for Foucault," Gerald Rabkin credits the influence of Foucault for what he considered a renewed interest in historical inquiry in theatre studies, following the relative ahistoricism of deconstruction, as well as with encouraging new approaches to such inquiry among scholars of both dramatic literature and performance. Indeed, not only have scholars in performance studies drawn on Foucault's analyses of the development of prisons, hospitals, sexuality, power, and physical discipline to inform their own examinations of specific kinds of cultural performance, such as surgical and anatomical demonstrations (see Thacker), public executions (see Conquergood), and political performance (see Erickson), but also some employ Foucault's genealogical approach themselves by looking for hitherto unnoticed connections within particular historical archives. Thacker's work on the public exposure of the body is notable in this context, as is Shannon Jackson's *Professing Performance*, in which she turns a Foucauldian eye on the development of theatre and performance as objects of academic scrutiny and the "disciplining" first of theatre, then of performance studies.

Further reading

By Foucault

"About the Beginning of the Hermeneutics of the Self." In *Religion and Culture*. Edited by Jeremy R. Carette. London: Routledge, 1999.

The Archaeology of Knowledge. Translated by A.M. Sheridan-Smith. London: Tavistock, 1974

The Birth of the Clinic: An Archaeology of Medical Perception. Translated by A.M. Sheridan-Smith. New York: Pantheon, 1973.

The History of Sexuality, Volume I: An Introduction. Translated by Robert Hurley. New York: Vintage, 1978.

Madness and Civilization: A History of Insanity in the Age of Reason. Translated by Richard Howard. New York: Vintage, 1973

*"Nietzsche, Genealogy, History." In *Language, Counter-memory, Practice: Selected Essays and Interviews*. Edited by Donald F. Bourchard. Ithaca, NY: Cornell University Press, 1977.

The Order of Things: An Archaeology of the Human Sciences. Translated by Alan Sheridan. New York: Vintage, 1970.

*"The Subject and Power." Afterword to *Michel Foucault: Beyond Structuralism and Hermeneutics*. Edited by Hubert L. Dreyfus and Paul Rabinow. Chicago, IL: University of Chicago Press, 1983.

"Technologies of the Self." In *The Essential Foucault*. Edited by Paul Rabinow and Nikolas Rose. New York: The New Press, 2003.

About Foucault

Conquergood, Dwight. "Lethal Theatre: Performance, Punishment, and the Death Penalty." *Theatre Journal* 54 (2002): 339–67.

Danaher, Geoff, Schirato, Tony, and Webb, Jen. *Understanding Foucault*. London: Sage, 2000.

Dreyfus, Hubert L., and Rabinow, Paul. *Michel Foucault: Beyond Structuralism and Hermeneutics*, 2nd edn. Chicago, IL: University of Chicago Press, 1983.

Erickson, Jon. "Defining Political Performance with Foucault and Habermas: Strategic and Communicative Action." In *Theatricality*. Edited by Tracy C. Davis and Thomas Postlewait. Cambridge: Cambridge University Press, 2003.

Jackson, Shannon. *Professing Performance: Theatre in the Academy from Philology to Performativity*. Cambridge: Cambridge University Press, 2004.

McNay, Lois. *Foucault and Feminism: Power, Gender and the Self*. Boston, MA: Northeastern University Press, 1992.

*Mills, Sara. *Michel Foucault*. London: Routledge, 2003.

Rabkin, Gerald. "Waiting for Foucault: New Theatre Theory." *Performing Arts Journal* 14, no. 3 (1992): 90–101.

Thacker, Eugene. "Performing the Technoscientific Body: RealVideo Surgery and the Anatomy Theatre." *Body and Society* 5, nos. 2–3 (1999): 317–36.

17 Hans-Georg Gadamer

Key concepts

- hermeneutics
- effective history
- fusion of horizons
- mimesis
- prejudice

Hans-Georg Gadamer (1900–2002) was born in Marburg, Germany. He studied philosophy and classical philology at the University of Marburg, and took his doctorate under the direction of Martin Heidegger in 1929. He held posts at the universities of Marburg, Leipzig, Frankfurt, and Heidelberg. Although he retired in 1968, he remained active in research and writing until his death in 2002. His complete collected works fill ten volumes.

Along with Heidegger and the philosopher of religion Paul Ricoeur, Gadamer is one of the most important twentieth-century scholars of **hermeneutics**, the science and art of interpretation, a field of study that has its ancient beginnings in scriptural studies. In Gadamer's work hermeneutics is transformed from the science of interpretation to the science of *understanding*. As such, it replaces metaphysics and epistemology as lords of the human sciences, addressing how humans find meaning and understand themselves and the world.

Gadamer's best known and most influential work is *Truth and Method* (published in German 1960, translated into English 1975). There he develops a theory of understanding as linguistic and historical. Understanding takes form in language, and its form would be different if it were to develop in another linguistic field or according to other terms. Language is not simply a tool one uses to communicate, but the medium in which one lives and moves and has one's being. There is no understanding of oneself or of another without language. One is born and raised and formed as a subject within a language. Indeed, language is "the house of being." Likewise, there is no such thing as understanding that is not rooted in a particular historical context. Following Heidegger's concept of Being as *Dasein*, "there-being,"

Gadamer insists that human being is always already located, that is, "here." Human existence is always being-in-the-world, and there is no way for a human being to eradicate that historical-cultural situatedness from her understanding of anything. Gadamer describes this historical and linguistic situatedness of the human being as a person's *Wirkungsgeschichte*, or **effective history**.

Yet there is another side to the hermeneutical event, another horizon. There is something – a work of art, a text, a cultural artifact, an idea – that is "other," that the human encounters and seeks to understand. Understanding is the process in which that "other" thing or idea or person is made meaningful, that is, understood. Gadamer describes this process of understanding as a **fusion of horizons**. On the one hand, there is the horizon of the one who wants to understand, located within that person's particular historical and linguistic context and shaped by its preexisting traditions, its effective history. On the other hand, there is the thing or person or text that someone is trying to understand. And that other horizon emerges from its own more or less unfamiliar historical and linguistic context. In the hermeneutical process, that is, the process of interpretation, the horizon of the interpreter fuses with that other horizon, creating a new dialogical meaning that is not identical to the monologue of the interpreter.

In his thoughts on our interactions with works of art, Gadamer redefined the concept of **mimesis**. Gadamer wished to challenge the modern separation of art from other aspects of life as the object of a distinct, contemplative attitude in favor of a view that sees the experience of art as more continuous with the rest of life. For Gadamer, mimesis resides not only in the way a particular text or work of art represents or imitates something, as classical definitions would have it, but also in the way we, as historically situated viewers or recipients of the work, interact with it. We interact with works of art that move us by discovering a truth through our engagement with them. This truth does not reside eternally in the work of art, waiting to be discovered through interpretation, but rather comes into being through the interaction of specific individuals with specific works in experiences that simultaneously reveal the work and the self. Mimesis is thus an active process through which we come to understand not only representations of the world, but also ourselves.

Gadamer's theory of understanding as historical and linguistic involves a critique of Enlightenment thought, with its ideal of the objective interpreter who remains detached from all cultural influences that threaten to **prejudice** her understanding. For Gadamer, there is no such thing as unprejudiced understanding. Understanding always involves pre-understanding. We are always already historically situated, shaped by our culture and language, and that situatedness shapes our understandings of everything. We bring our own horizon, our own effective history, as a prejudice to any moment of understanding. For Gadamer, "the prejudices of the individual, far more than his judgments, constitute the historical reality of his being" (*Truth and*

Method, p. 245). For this reason, Gadamer did not believe that historians, in particular, should pretend to be objective. Rather, they should acknowledge their prejudices and enter actively into dialogue with the horizon of the era whose story they seek to tell on that basis. The historical narrative that emerges reflects this interaction between historian and source material, both understood as historically situated and therefore reflective of prejudice.

Gadamer's rehabilitation of prejudice put his hermeneutical theory in direct conflict with the tradition of ideological critique, insofar as it suggested that there is no non-ideological position from which to critique an ideology. This made Gadamer appear to some that he was returning to a pre-critical position, and led to a now famous series of debates with Jürgen Habermas, who contended that Gadamer's position does not adequately recognize the ways ideology can distort communication through the hidden expression of force (see Ricoeur). He also argued that Gadamer places too much weight on the power of our historical and linguistic context as that which constitutes us. Habermas, by contrast, called for more of an orientation toward the future, with an emancipatory interest in what ought to be rather than what was and is.

Gadamer's ideas about history have implications for all historical discourses and have been considered by historians of performance concerned to transcend the limitations of supposedly objective, positivistic approaches to the writing of history. Another area in which Gadamer's ideas have important implications is in the consideration of what it means to recreate historical performances. What is the objective of such activity and can it be met? For example, can musicians really develop a "period ear" (see Burstyn) that allows them to hear music of bygone eras the same way that the musicians of those eras did and, therefore, to perform the music authentically? Gadamer's philosophy suggests that claims to be able to recreate vanished performance styles or restage historical performances accurately from documentation are deeply suspect – approaching such work from the point of view of precipitating a new understanding from the synthesis of the work's original historical horizon with the present horizon seems more fruitful.

Further reading

By Gadamer

Philosophical Hermeneutics. Edited by David E. Linge. Berkeley, CA: University of California Press, 1976.

"Text and Interpretation." Translated by Dennis J. Schmidt. In *Hermeneutics and Modern Philosophy*. Edited by Brice R. Wachterhauser, pp. 377–96. Albany, NY: State University of New York Press, 1986.

Truth and Method, 2nd revised edn. Translated by Garrett Barden and John Cumming. Revised translation by Joel Weinsheimer and Donald G. Marshall. New York: Crossroad, 1993.

About Gadamer

Brooks, Lynn Matluck. "Dance History and Method: A Return to Meaning." *Dance Research: Journal of the Society for Dance Research* 20, no. 1 (2002): 33–53.

Burstyn, Shai. "In Quest of the Period Ear." *Early Music* 25, no. 4 (1997): 692–701.

Grondin, Jean. "Gadamer's Aesthetics: The Overcoming of Aesthetic Consciousness and the Hermeneutical Art of Truth." In *Encyclopedia of Aesthetics*, vol. 2. Edited by Michael Kelly. New York: Oxford University Press, 1998.

McConachie, Bruce. "Towards a Postpositivist Theatre History." *Theatre Journal* 37, no. 4 (1985): 465–86.

*Ricoeur, Paul. "Hermeneutics and the Critique of Ideology." In *Hermeneutics and Modern Philosophy*. Edited by Brice R. Wachterhauser. Albany, NY: State University of New York Press, 1986.

Schweiker, William. "Beyond Imitation: Aesthetic Praxis in Gadamer, Ricoeur, and Derrida." *Journal of Religion* 68, no. 1 (1988): 21–38.

18 Luce Irigaray

Key concepts

- sexual difference
- specul(ariz)ation
- critical mimesis

Luce Irigaray was born in Belgium in 1930. She earned her master's degree from the University of Louvain in 1955 and then taught high school in Brussels until 1959. She moved to Paris where she earned a master's (1961) and then a diploma (1962) in psychology from the University of Paris. She attended Jacques LACAN's seminars, became a member of his École freudienne de Paris, and trained to become an analyst. In 1968 she also received her doctorate in linguistics, which led to a teaching position at the University of Vincennes (1970–74). She was expelled from Jacques Lacan's École and lost her faculty post at Vincennes after publishing *Speculum of the Other Woman* (1974), which was her second doctoral thesis. She is currently Director of Research at the Centre national de la recherche scientifique (CNRS) in Paris.

Unlike some other French feminists with whom she is frequently identified (especially KRISTEVA), Irigaray has consistently held that there is in fact such a thing as **sexual difference** and that female sexual identity is autonomous and unique, grounded in women's specific embodied experiences (a position sometimes called "difference feminism").

In *Speculum of the Other Woman* and other early works such as *This Sex Which is Not One* (collected essays first published in 1977), she argues that western intellectual tradition has essentially elided the feminine, positing it not on its own terms but rather in relation to, or rather over against, the masculine as the normative human identity. "Woman" in western discourse has largely been defined as man's other. Mimicking the discourses of FREUD, Plato, and other intellectuals writing "about women" – What are they? Where do they come from? What are they for? – she demonstrates how "woman" functions primarily as an idea that clarifies "man," that is, man's other/opposite. She describes this in terms of a process of **specul(ariz)ation**, that is, a process of male speculation about woman as man's other that associates her with a series of other terms and concepts within a larger set of oppositions that organize the western patriarchal symbolic order (on which see LACAN in this volume). Within this set of structural oppositions or "interpretive modalities" that shape our understanding of the world, woman and the feminine are associated in each pairing with the negative terms: light/ dark, in/out, heavens/earth, and especially phallus/lack, original/derivative, positive/negative, and active/passive.

> All these are interpretive modalities of the female function rigorously postulated by the pursuit of a certain game for which she will always find herself signed up without having begun to play. . . . A reserve supply of negativity sustaining the articulation of their moves, or refusals to move, in a partly fictional progress toward the mastery of power.
> (*Speculum of the Other Woman*, p. 22)

Elsewhere she states: "The 'feminine' is always described in terms of deficiency or atrophy, as the other side of the sex that alone holds monopoly on value: the male sex" (*This Sex Which is Not One*, p. 69).

Working against this symbolic reduction of woman to the "other side" of man, Irigaray asserts the non-oppositional difference of a real embodied other woman. Here woman is not reducible to man's other/opposite; her otherness refuses to be reduced to an object of exchange within the male sexual economy. This is an otherness with agency that is unpredictable and irreducible to the male economy. As such, her voice, action, and way of seeing (as opposed to her being talked about, acted upon, and seen) have subversive power within that economy to bring about a "disaggregation" of the privileged male/masculine subject of western discourse and society (*Speculum of the Other Woman*, p. 135). Thus woman's subjectivity, as other, can bring about a collapse of the binary logic of the male symbolic order, thereby opening up new possibilities of social relations.

This characterization of female subjectivity has led to accusations of essentialism against Irigaray. She insists, however, that she envisions an autonomous female identity as something toward which to strive, not something that is actually achievable. "In order to become," she writes, "it is essential to have a gender or an essence . . . as horizon. . . . To become means fulfilling the wholeness of what we are capable of being. Obviously, this road never ends" (*Sexes and Genealogies*, p. 61). This last sentence is crucial for the way it suggests that a reified notion of gender identity is not an end toward which to strive but a means to sustain an ongoing process of becoming that never reaches a defined goal.

The aspect of Irigaray's thought to have the most impact on performance studies is her concept of **critical mimesis**. Because any distinctly feminine identity women might claim will be recuperated by and for masculine hegemony, women have to adopt subversive strategies for being seen or heard at all. Critical mimesis is the strategy of undermining dominant masculine discourses neither by positing equivalent feminine positions from which to speak nor by claiming to take up a position that is altogether outside of gendered discourse, but rather by mimicking the dominant discourse to bore away at it from within. This is not the same thing as parody, which always suggests a defined position from which one critiques that which one imitates. As described by Irigaray in a famous passage from *This Sex Which is Not One*, worth quoting at length, the strategy is closer to a specifically feminist form of deconstruction in that it hopes to subtly reveal the traces of repressed discourses that were always already present in the dominant:

> There is . . . perhaps only one "path," the one historically assigned to the feminine: that of mimicry. One must assume the feminine role deliberately. Which means already to convert a form of subordination into an affirmation, and thus to begin to thwart it. Whereas a direct feminine challenge to this condition means demanding to speak as a (masculine) "subject". . . . To play with mimesis is thus, for a woman, to try to recover the place of her exploitation by discourse, without allowing her to be simply reduced to it. It means to resubmit herself . . . to "ideas," in particular to ideas about herself, that are elaborated in/by a masculine logic, but so as to make "visible," by an effect of playful repetition what was supposed to remain invisible: the cover-up of a possible operation of the feminine in language. It also means to "unveil" the fact that, if women are such good mimics, it is because they are not simply resorbed in this function. *They also remain elsewhere.*
> (*This Sex Which is Not One*, p. 76; emphasis in original)

Women embrace a position assigned to them by masculine discourse, that of mimics, only to simultaneously dismantle that discourse and show that they cannot be reduced to it. It is important that the "elsewhere" to which Irigaray alludes remain undefined (though she does discuss some possible conceptualizations of it) so that it does not become a reified feminine identity. In rhetorical terms, Irigraray's notion of critical mimesis somewhat resembles both Slavoj ŽIŽEK's concept of "over-identification" with the dominant discourse as a critical act and Gayatri SPIVAK's concept of "strategic essentialism." It has proved valuable as a model for theorizing feminist performance strategies as well as a critical frame to analyze specific performances. It has also been extended to other identity categories: perhaps there are instances in which people of color employ critical mimesis to undermine the dominant white discourse and their position within it, for example.

Further reading

By Irigaray

Sexes and Genealogies. Translated by Gillian C. Gill. Ithaca, NY: Cornell University Press, 1993.

*Speculum of the Other Woman. Translated by Gillian C. Gill. Ithaca, NY: Cornell University Press, 1985.

*This Sex Which is Not One. Translated by Catherine Porter. Ithaca, NY: Cornell University Press, 1985.

About Irigaray

Diamond, Elin. *Unmaking Mimesis: Essays on Feminism and Theater*. London: Routledge, 1997.

Fuchs, Elinor. "Postmodernism and the Scene of Theater." In *The Death of Character: Perspectives on Theater after Modernism*. Bloomington, IN: University of Indiana Press, 1996.

Gilson-Ellis, Jools. "Mouth Ghosts: The Taste of the *Os-Text*." In *Languages of Theatre Shaped by Women*. Edited by Lizbeth Goodman and Jane de Gay. Bristol: Intellect Books, 2000.

Gingrich-Philbrook, Craig. "Love's Excluded Subjects: Staging Irigaray's Heteronormative Essentialism." *Cultural Studies* 15, no. 2 (2001): 222–28.

Hamera, Judith. "I Dance to You: Reflections on Irigaray's *I Love to You* in Pilates and Virtuosity." *Cultural Studies* 15, no. 2 (2001): 229–40.

*Huffer, Lynne. "Luce et Veritas: Toward an Ethics of Performance." *Yale French Studies* 87 (1995): 20–41.

Pizzato, Mark. "Genet's Dismemberment through Lacan's Orders and Irigaray's Cave." In *Edges of Loss: From Modern Drama to Postmodern Theory*. Ann Arbor, MI: University of Michigan Press, 1998.

Shimakawa, Karen. "Swallowing the Tempest: Asian American Women on Stage." *Theatre Journal* 47, no. 3 (1995): 367–80.

19 Julia Kristeva

Key concepts

- intertextuality
- semiotic, *chora*
- signifying process
- subject in process
- abjection

Julia Kristeva (1941–) is a psychoanalysist and feminist theorist of language and literature. Born in Bulgaria, she moved to Paris in 1966 on a doctoral research fellowship. There she quickly became involved in the leftist intellectual movement that congregated around the literary journal *Tel Quel*. Her most influential teacher during that time was Roland BARTHES. Her doctoral thesis, *Revolution in Poetic Language* (published in 1974) led to her appointment to a chair in linguistics at the University of Paris VII, where she has remained throughout her academic career. Since 1979 she has also maintained a practice as a psychoanalyst.

Kristeva works at the intersection of linguistics, psychoanalysis, and feminist theory. She has written on numerous topics, from horror to love to depression. Overall, her interests lie less in the formal structures of language and meaning than in what escapes and disrupts – the unrepresentable, inexpressible other within language, within the self, and within society. There she sees the possibility for revolutionary social transformation.

Kristeva's theory of **intertextuality** has had a tremendous influence on literary studies, and to some extent on performance studies. This theory was developed in relation to Mikhail BAKHTIN's concept of dialogism. The idea of intertextuality first appears in her 1969 essay, "Word, Dialogue and the Novel," as part of a larger critique of modern conceptions of texts as discrete, self-enclosed containers of meaning. Contrary to this conception, intertextuality draws attention to the fact that every text is "constructed as a mosaic of quotations" ("Word, Dialogue, and Novel," p. 66). It is a "field of transpositions of various signifying systems (an inter-textuality)" (*Revolution in Poetic Language*, p. 60), an "*intersection of textual surfaces* rather than a point (a fixed meaning)" ("Word, Dialogue, and Novel," p. 65; emphasis in original).

In *Revolution in Poetic Language*, Kristeva refers to the potentially revolutionary otherness within language as the **semiotic**, or *chora*, which is in tension with the symbolic, or *thetic*. This semiotic is decipherable within language (especially in poetic language) yet it is in tension with the dominant symbolic order (on which see LACAN) that governs language. In psychoanalytic terms, the semiotic or *chora* is associated with the prelinguistic phase and the mother's body. Indeed, Kristeva associates this choratic element in poetic language with the mother, the child, prelinguistic babbling, and so on (see particularly her early memoir of motherhood, "Stabat Mater"). It exists within language, especially poetic language, as a potentially subversive force. The semiotic can never be entirely constrained by the symbolic; it perpetually infiltrates the symbolic construction of meaning and so reintroduces fluidity and heterogeneity within the speaking / writing subject. It reopens the process of creation. Kristeva describes it as the "very precondition" of symbolic order (*Revolution in Poetic Language*, p. 50). Insofar as the symbolic order of language is identified with consciousness, we can think of the semiotic or *chora* as language's unconscious. The infiltration of the semiotic within language is the return of the linguistically repressed. Notice that Kristeva's concept of the semiotic differs from its standard meaning of semiotics as the science of signs.

In *Revolution in Poetic Language* and other works, Kristeva focuses on the **signifying process** more than its product. She reads a text in order to discover not only the processes by which it comes to gain meaning (*signify*) but also what within the text resists and undermines that process (see also Kristeva's "Semiotics" and "The System and the Speaking Subject"). In this respect, we can think of her method of literary analysis as a kind of psychoanalysis of texts, not taking their final, fixed state for granted but looking into them in order to explore how they came into being, how they came to say what they say, as well as what was repressed in the process and what within them keeps them fundamentally unstable. In this way her analysis seeks those places in language that open to the possibility of social transformation, "the production of a different kind of subject, one capable of bringing about new social relations, and thus joining in the process of capitalism's subversion" (*Revolution in Poetic Language*, p. 105).

Kristeva's approach to the ideas of identity and subject formation likewise emphasizes continual process rather than stability. Just as the invisible presence of the semiotic beneath the symbolic destabilizes language as a determined signifying system and just as texts mean what they do not say as much as what they do, so too human subjects are, in Kristeva's view, finally elusive and always **subjects in process**. "Kristeva presents a subject which is never entirely analysable, but rather one always incomplete: the subject as the impetus for an infinite series of elaborations" (John Lechte, "Julia Kristeva," p. 143).

Although Kristeva's work is feminist in its focus on the status of femininity within social systems of signification, she has been highly critical of feminism as a movement. She has written a great deal about the social and political oppression and exclusion of women but her thinking runs counter to some of the main tendencies in feminism. For one thing, she considers sexual difference to be "at once biological, physiological, and relative to reproduction" ("Women's Time," p. 21) not just socially constructed (as Judith BUTLER suggests, for example). For another, she resists identity politics precisely because she resists the notion of identity itself. In the conclusion to "Women's Time," an essay surveying the development of feminism (originally published in French in 1979), Kristeva proposes a new way of thinking in which

> the very dichotomy man/woman as an opposition between two rival entities may be understood as belonging to *metaphysics*. What can "identity," even "sexual identity," mean in a new theoretical and scientific space in which the very notion of identity is challenged?
>
> ("Women's Time," pp. 33–34; emphasis in original)

Ultimately, she is interested in discursive practices that focus on each person as an individual, rather than as a member of a category, and can "bring out – along with the multiplicity of every person's possible identifications . . . *the relativity of his/her symbolic as well as biological existence*, according to the variation in his/her symbolic capacities" ("Women's Time," p. 35; emphasis in original).

Another key concept in Kristeva's work is **abjection** (see especially *Powers of Horror*, first published in French in 1980). The abject is that which does not fit within the social and symbolic order of things, and which therefore must be excluded from that order, declared unclean or impure and pushed outside the boundaries. Always threatening to break back into that order and contaminate it, the abject must be kept at bay. Abjection, then, is the process by which a society identifies the abject and excludes it from its order through various prohibitions and taboos. As such, abjection serves to define the boundaries of the social-symbolic order. Within this system, "the pure will be that which conforms to an established taxonomy" and the impure, or abject, will be "that which unsettles it, establishes intermixture and disorder" (*Powers of Horror*, p. 99).

Although Kristeva has pointed specifically to "aesthetic practices" as means of disrupting the social and linguistic status quo ("Women's Time," p. 34), she has expressed doubts about the theatre's ability to do this. Writing in 1977, Kristeva posits that "modern theatre does not exist – it does not take (a) place" ("Modern Theatre," p. 131) by which she means that the theatre, excluded from its traditional social function in the modern world, has not discovered a new purpose for itself and ends up either reinforcing the dominant ideology or catering to a small, self-selected audience.

She also argues that theatre and film are no longer distinguishable in terms of their social and representational functions. In spite of this skepticism with respect to the theatre, Kristeva's ideas have been taken up within theatre and performance studies. For some writers, the inchoate realm of meaning she calls the semiotic or *chora* is accessible through performance, perhaps even the realm in which performance per se (as opposed to written texts) operates. Actors and other kinds of performers can be seen as plunging into and exploring that pre-discursive realm through their artistic processes. Kristeva's concept of abjection has also proved fruitful. Whereas some writers use it to describe the representational status of marginalized social groups in performance, others argue that performance itself can be seen as abject: a socially suspect practice whose strength may reside in its ability to agitate the symbolic.

Further reading

By Kristeva

*The Kristeva Reader. Edited by Toril Moi. New York: Columbia University Press, 1986.

"Modern Theatre Does Not Take (a) Place." Translated by Alice Jardine and Thomas Gora. *SubStance*, 18–19 (1977): 131–34.

Powers of Horror: An Essay on Abjection. Translated by L.S. Roudiez. New York: Columbia University Press, 1982.

Revolution in Poetic Language. Abridged and translated by Margaret Waller. New York: Columbia University Press, 1984.

"Semiotics: A Critical Science and/or a Critique of Science." In *The Kristeva Reader*. Edited by Toril Moi. New York: Columbia University Press, 1986.

"Stabat Mater." In *The Kristeva Reader*. Edited by Toril Moi. New York: Columbia University Press, 1986.

"The System and the Speaking Subject." In *The Kristeva Reader*. Edited by Toril Moi. New York: Columbia University Press, 1986.

Tales of Love. Translated by L.S. Roudiez. New York: Columbia University Press, 1987.

"Women's Time." Translated by Alice Jardine and Henry Blake. *Signs* 7, no.1 (1981): 13–35.

"Word, Dialogue and the Novel." In *Desire in Language: A Semiotic Approach to Literature and Art*. Edited by Leon Roudiez. New York: Columbia University Press, 1980.

About Kristeva

Boenisch, Peter. "www dot theatre dot. Alice Croft, or: Transforming Performance in the Internet Culture." *Body, Space and Technology* 2, no. 2 (2002). Online, available at: http://people.brunel.ac.uk/bst/vol0202/index.html

Bryant-Bertail, Sara. "The True-Real Woman: Maddy Roony as *Picara* in *All That Fall*." *ASSAPH – Studies in the Theatre* 11 (1993). Online, available at: www.tau.ac.il/arts/publications/ASSAPHTH11/BERTAIL.html

Diamond, Elin. "Refusing the Romance of Identity: Narrative Interventions in Churchill, Benmussa, Duras." *Theatre Journal* 37, no. 3 (1985): 273–86.

Jardine, Alice. "Introduction to Julia Kristeva's 'Women's Time'." *Signs* 7, no. 1 (1981): 5–12.

Jürs-Munby, Karen. "Of Textual Bodies and Actual Bodies: The Abjection of Performance in Lessing's Dramaturgy." *Theatre Research International* 30, no. 1 (2004): 19–35.

Lechte, John. *Julia Kristeva*. London: Routledge, 1990.

Lechte, John. "Julia Kristeva." In *Fifty Key Contemporary Thinkers*. London: Routledge, 1991.

Pizzato, Mark. "Brecht's Repression of the Kristevan *Chora*." In *Edges of Loss: From Modern Drama to Postmodern Theory*. Ann Arbor, MI: University of Michigan Press, 1998.

Shimakawa, Karen. *National Abjection: The Asian American Body on Stage*. Durham, NC: Duke University Press, 2002.

20 Jacques Lacan

Key concepts

- symbolic order
- unconscious
- Real
- Imaginary
- mirror stage
- desire
- phallus, castration
- the gaze
- split subjectivity

Jacques Lacan (1901–81) was born in Paris to a Catholic family. He earned a medical degree at the Sorbonne and then trained as a psychoanalyst. His relationship with mainstream psychoanalysis in Europe was tense, and he resigned from the Société psychanalytique de Paris in 1953 – the same year he gave his famous lecture "The Function and Field of Speech and Language" at the International Psychoanalytic Association in Rome (also referred to as "The Rome Discourse"). It was also that same year that he inaugurated his weekly seminar, which continued almost until his death in 1981. Lacan's seminar was the primary venue for sharing his work. Most of his published essays were originally given as papers in this seminar, which was attended by many intellectuals, including Julia KRISTEVA and Luce IRIGARAY. In 1963, he founded the École freudienne de Paris.

Focused on the formation of the subject and the role of the unconscious, Lacan's work constitutes a radical reinterpretation of FREUD and psychoanalysis in light of structuralism (especially the structural linguistics of SAUSSURE and the structural anthropology of Lévi-Strauss). Dissenting from the common conception, widespread among his contemporaries (and championed especially by Heinz Hartmann), of the ego or conscious self as autonomous, sovereign, and biologically determined, Lacan theorized that it was formed within a pre-existing symbolic order, interpolated within a system of meaning that it had no part in creating. Far from autonomous and sovereign, it becomes a subject, an ego, an "I," when it is *subjected* to a pre-existing **symbolic order**. The **unconscious**, moreover, is not a biologically determined realm of libidinal drives; rather, it is formed in tandem with the formation of ego. It is a side-effect of the ego's subjection within the symbolic order. It is created as the excess, the surplus of self that does not fit within the subject as it is formed by the symbolic order. Thus the unconscious reveals the fact that we as subjects are always more and other than our social selves allow. The unconscious reveals our "toomuchness," the fact that we are split selves. Far from being an autonomous, sovereign agent in the world, then, the ego is an illusion, a symbolically constructed selfhood whose excesses, splits, and gaps are revealed by the eruptions of the unconscious into conscious life.

Lacan develops this understanding of ego formation and the unconscious vis-à-vis the structural linguistics of Saussure. For Lacan, the birth of subjectivity is one's entry into language, understood as a synchronic system of signs and social codes that generate meaning, that is, a symbolic order. It is this symbolic order that locates you, forms you, "subjects" you, thereby enabling you to become an acting subject. Before Lacan, most psychoanalysts believed that the development of the ego as the seat of consciousness was a biological development. Lacan argued that it was a linguistic-symbolic development. Birth into language is birth into subjectivity. As he famously pronounced in "The Function and Field of Speech and Language," "Man speaks, then, but it is because the symbol has made him man" (p. 65). And later in the same essay,

> Symbols in fact envelop the life of man in a network so total that they join together, before he comes into the world, those who are going to engender him "by flesh and blood"; so total that they bring to his birth, along with the gifts of the stars, if not with the gifts of the fairies, the shape of his destiny; so total that they give the words that will make him faithful or renegade, the law of the acts that will follow him right to the very place where he *is* not yet and even beyond his death; and so total that through them his end finds its meaning in the last judgment, where the Word absolves his being or condemns it.
>
> ("The Function and Field of Speech and Language," p. 68)

The subject emerges from its non-individuated, prelinguistic state of being not into unmediated reality but into a culturally constructed world of symbols, a symbolic order. The subject is constituted by the symbolic order, which has, as Slavoj ŽIŽEK puts it, colonized the live body like a parasite (*The Fragile Absolute*, p. 91). Although conscious human existence is thus culturally constructed through language, the subject does not recognize it as such, but experiences (or rather imagines) it to be reality itself.

Lacan uses the term **Real** in reference to that which is really "there", "in its place" apart from the symbolic order and outside its ordering of things. It is the present, as opposed to that which is re-presented through language in the symbolic order. The human subject, constituted by the symbolic order, is radically alienated from the Real. As such, it is unattainable.

A crucial stage in this development, according to Lacan, is the subject's entry into the **Imaginary**, which is closely related to the mirror stage (for a clear discussion of both, see "The Mirror Stage as Formative of the Function of the I as Revealed in Psychoanalytic Experience," first presented in 1949). The Imaginary precedes the child's entry into the symbolic order and continues to operate along with it throughout one's life. The Imaginary is the order according to which the child becomes aware of itself as an "I," a subject, among other subjects. It is the general matrix of self and other.

Lacan identifies the **mirror stage** as an important means by which the child is inaugurated into the Imaginary. The mirror stage occurs between the ages of 6 and 18 months, when the child first recognizes itself in a mirror as a coherent whole self, like other selves. In this moment, before the child can speak or even walk, the child recognizes itself as an "I." Yet this recognition is in fact a mis-recognition, for it is a recognition of itself *as other*, an objec-tification of itself in an image whose point of view and position are outside itself. In this respect the mirror stage, which inaugurates the Imaginary, may be seen as "one of those crises of alienation around which the Lacanian subject is organized, since to know oneself through an external image is to be defined through self-alienation" (Silverman, *The Subject of* Semiotics, p. 158).

According to Lacan's narrative of child development, the child's entry into language as a subject coincides with its separation from the mother. The mother, therefore, is the child's first experience of lack – absence – which creates the condition of **desire**. The father intervenes in the mother–child relationship at a moment coinciding with the child's entry into the symbolic order and loss of union with the mother. As the child becomes a subject within the symbolic order, the father is identified with that order which constitutes and governs subjectivity. For this reason Lacan sometimes called the symbolic order *le Nom-du-Père* ("the Name of the Father") which in French is pronounced the same as *le Non-du-Père* ("the No of the Father"), thus signifying God-like authority and prohibition. Thus the child is *subjected* in both senses of the word: subjected to the law of the symbolic order (identified with patriarchal law/no of the father), and constituted as a subject acting in the world.

This is where the **phallus** comes in, so to speak. One of the first childhood experiences of sexual difference for the child, according to Lacan as well as Freud, is the recognition that the mother does not have a penis. But for Lacan, what is most important is the *symbolic* significance of the penis, a significance he emphasizes by consistently using the term "phallus." What matters in the symbolic order is not the body part, but what it signifies. First, it signifies sexual difference. Second, insofar as the father (identified with the symbolic order) has a penis and the mother (identified with the prelinguistic state of bliss before entry into the symbolic order) does not, the phallus signifies lack/absence within the symbolic order. For Lacan, the phallus comes to signify *both* women's and men's lack, dependence, and subjective vulnerability within the symbolic order. The father may be identified by the child with the symbolic, but he too was once a child, subjected to the same law and always inadequate and incomplete in relation to it, never in full possession of it. No one possesses the phallus. All are "**castrated.**"

Some scholars of gender find Lacan useful because he insists that there is nothing essential about the androcentric symbolic order with its foundational patriarchal structures of sexual difference. For Lacan, there is nothing essential or "natural" about sexual difference itself. Woman, man, femininity, and masculinity are symbolic constructions, formed arbitrarily by a repressive system of meaning that masquerades as the Real.

As mentioned earlier, the unconscious is formed at the same time as the subject/ego. It is an effect of the repression that takes place during subjection. Ego formation requires repression of whatever does not fit within the symbolic order – whatever exceeds it. The unconscious is "the censored chapter" in the history of psychic life ("The Function and Field of Speech and Language," p. 50). It is an otherness within – in Freudian terms, the *unheimlich*, the "unhomely" that remains, closeted, in the home of selfhood – manifesting itself in and through language, often as interruption – mispeakings, slips, and forgetting names. And when it does so it pokes holes in the subject and its world, potentially revealing its illusory nature. In other words, the in-breaking of the unconscious within conscious existence reveals the fact that the subject is a tentative construction, by no means entirely stable or permanent and not entirely whole. In Lacan's words, "the unconscious is that part of the concrete discourse . . . that is not at the disposal of the subject in re-establishing the continuity of his conscious discourse" ("The Function and Field of Speech and Language," p. 49). It is an in-breaking that may open one's consciousness to the possibility that the Real is elsewhere, lost beyond one's grasp.

Lacanian psychoanalysis has been influential on performance studies largely because of his hypothesis of the mirror stage, which has been taken up as a way of understanding and linking the concepts of identity, subjectivity, and spectatorship. For Lacan, identity formation at the mirror stage is a process that takes place through interaction (even if only at an imaginary level) rather than a biological given or something that develops autonomously – in that sense, subjectivity is anchored in spectatorship. Lacan's model for the formation of the self thus relates broadly to the interactionist turn in sociology represented by the work of Erving Goffman and others for whom identity is always enacted in relation to forces and people outside oneself (albeit at a social rather than psychological level). Judith BUTLER has drawn frequently on Lacan in formulating her concept of gender identity as a performative – as opposed to genetic or physiological – structure into which individuals are incorporated socially through language.

The mirror stage also models relationships between aesthetic performances and their audiences, as Laura Mulvey, a film theorist whose work has impacted on performance studies, was one of the first to suggest. In her well-known 1975 essay "Visual Pleasure and Narrative Cinema," Mulvey uses the mirror stage as a heuristic for examining the gender politics inherent in the way traditional narrative films construct spectatorship: "the image of woman as (passive) raw material for the (active) **gaze** of man" (p. 493). Herbert Blau also draws on Lacan in trying to understand the complexity of theatre spectatorship, which is driven by desire, subjectivity, and scopophilia. Blau describes Lacan's scenario of the mirror stage as both "a miniature drama" and "an initial act of spectatorship" (Blau, *The Audience*, p. 65). Finally, Matthew Causey, in "The Screen Test of the Double," carried this question into the era of mediatized performance, using the mirror stage and its attendant notion of **split subjectivity** (the subject's awareness of itself looking at itself) to analyze the ubiquity of screened images in postmodern performance and society. It is clear that Lacanian psychoanalysis offers to performance studies a rich matrix for thinking through issues of subjectivity, whether in the formation and performance of identity or performance–audience relationships.

Further reading

By Lacan

"The Agency of the Letter in the Unconscious or Reason since Freud." In *Ecrits: A Selection*. Translated by Alan Sheridan. London: Tavistock, 1977.

Four Fundamental Concepts of Psychoanalysis. Translated by Alan Sheridan. New York: Norton, 1978.

* "The Function and Field of Speech and Language in Psychoanalysis." In *Ecrits: A Selection*. Translated by Alan Sheridan. London: Tavistock, 1977.

* "The Mirror Stage as Formative of the Function of the I as Revealed in Psychoanalytic Experience." In *Ecrits: A Selection*. Translated by Alan Sheridan. London: Tavistock, 1977.

"The Signification of the Phallus." In *Ecrits: A Selection*. Translated by Alan Sheridan. London: Tavistock, 1977.

About Lacan

*Blau, Herbert. *The Audience*. Baltimore, MD: Johns Hopkins University Press, 1990.

*Butler, Judith. *Gender Trouble: Feminism and the Subversion of Identity*. New York: Routledge, 1990.

Causey, Matthew. "The Screen Test of the Double: The Uncanny Performer in the Space of Technology." In *Performance: Critical Concepts*, Vol. IV. Edited by Philip Auslander. London: Routledge, 2003. Originally published in *Theatre Journal* 51 (1999): 383–94.

*Evans, Dylan. *Introductory Dictionary of Lacanian Psychoanalysis*. New York: Routledge,1996.

Freedman, Barbara. "Frame-Up: Feminism, Psychoanalysis, Theatre." In *Performance: Critical Concepts*, Vol. II. Edited by Philip Auslander. London: Routledge, 2003. Originally published in *Theatre Journal* 40 (1988): 375–97.

Kubiak, Anthony. "Disappearance as History: The Stages of Terror." In *Performance: Critical Concepts*, Vol. III. Edited by Philip Auslander. London: Routledge, 2003. Originally published in *Theatre Journal* 39 (1987): 78–88.

Mulvey, Laura. "Visual Pleasure and Narrative Cinema." In *Film and Theory: An Anthology*. Edited by Robert Stam and Toby Miller. Malden, MA: Blackwell, 2000.

Phelan, Peggy. *Unmarked: The Politics of Performance*. London: Routledge, 1993.

Silverman, Kaja. *The Subject of Semiotics*. Oxford: Oxford University Press, 1983.

21 Henri Lefebvre

Key concepts

- everyday life
- perceived space
- conceived space
- lived space

Henri Lefebvre (1901–91) was a French Marxist social theorist, philosopher, and historian. Born and raised in the Landes region of southwestern France, he studied philosophy in Paris where he became involved with a group of young intellectuals promoting Marxist ideas. He joined the French Communist Party in 1928. He was influenced by Marx's early writings, some of which he translated into French. He fought in the French Resistance during World War II. Afterwards he became a broadcaster and devoted his time to writing about Marxism, though he regularly skirmished with the Party over his "humanist" Marxist views that were based, in part, on the Hegel-influenced early writings of Marx. Lefebvre was expelled from the French Communist Party in 1958 because of his anti-Stalinist views (though he became involved again in the late 1970s).

Later, in the 1950s, Lefebvre was appointed to a research position in sociology. It was during this time that he applied Marxist ideas to the sociology of everyday life. He went on to hold sociology chairs, first at Strasbourg and then at Nanterre, from which he played an active role in the 1968 Paris protests. It was during this period that he explored new intellectual currents, embracing ideas taken from sociology, literary criticism, and philosophy.

Lefebvre was antagonistic toward the linguistic and anthropological structuralisms popular among French intellectuals in the 1960s, and wrote articles criticizing the work of Claude Lévi-Strauss and Michel Foucault. He also critiqued the anti-humanist Marxist views of Louis Althusser, accusing him of turning structuralism into an ideology.

Lefebvre was the author of more than sixty books, although much of this work has yet to be translated into English. His scholarship has influenced such diverse disciplines as philosophy, sociology, literature, geography, and political science, and has been championed by postmodern spatial theorists among others. Lefebvre's major intellectual contributions concern the study of "everyday life" and the configuration of social space in capitalist urban settings.

In his own lifetime, Lefebvre was witness to the rise of industrialism in France and, along with it, the increasing urbanization and suburbanization of French life. These experiences informed his application of Marxist critical theory to problems of **everyday life**. Lefebvre draws attention to the social forms of alienation that appear in the quotidian affairs of human beings as a result of capitalist modernization. For Lefebvre, this alienation is the product of a three-stage process. In the first stage, everyday human activities are spontaneously ordered and largely independent of the state. This spontaneity is then co-opted in the second stage by capitalist forms of rational structure. Finally, in the third stage, these co-opted forms of everyday activity become systems of oppression. Economically, Lefebvre argues, divisions of labor become means for worker exploitation. Similarly, benign political structures become oppressive State ideologies.

In the three volumes of *Critique of Everyday Life* (the first volume was published in French in 1958), Lefebvre delineates the alienating effects of capitalism and urbanization on everyday life. He argues that within capitalist society, human beings lose control of their own self-actualization (as subjects) and increasingly describe themselves as objects within the economic system (as, for instance, "assets" and "consumers"). They objectify and commodify themselves in economic terms and thus become alienated from their own lives.

In *The Production of Space* (1974), Lefebvre turned his critical attention to an analysis of social space. He is concerned not only with how social space is produced within a social context, but also with how particular forms of space actually produce the forms of life that take place within them. Space is not simply an external location that human occupants act upon and shape, as we so often assume. Rather, space is a subject that acts upon and shapes us and our social lives.

Lefebvre reads space primarily from a Marxist perspective. He is interested in transcending a bipartite view of space as physical form – **perceived space** – and mental construct – **conceived space**. To this end, Lefebvre proposes a three-tiered analysis of space, one which adds a dimension that he refers to as **lived space**. Lefebvre organizes his trivalent spatial analysis in the following way:

> The fields we are concerned with are, first, the *physical* – nature, the Cosmos; secondly, the *mental*, including logical and formal abstractions; and, thirdly, the *social*. In other words, we are concerned with logico-epistemological space, the space of social practice, the space occupied by sensory phenomena, including products of the imagination such as projects and projections, symbols and utopias.
>
> (*The Production of Space*, pp. 11–12; emphases in original)

This tripartite view of space is understood *not* as three compartmentalized spaces – space separable into three – but is conceived as a synthesis of all three. All territory is comprised of all three aspects of space at once. Lefebvre charts his view of space in terms of the interconnections between the three categories of space. The table summarizes the terms he uses to name these three kinds of space along with the meaning assigned to these terms.

Edward Soja, in *Thirdspace* (1996) has taken up Lefebvre's spatial trialectics, developing his three categories in terms of Firstspace, Secondspace, and Thirdspace. For Soja, Thirdspace (Lefebvre's lived space) is a combination of Firstspace (perceived space) and Secondspace (conceived space). Thirdspace, then, cannot be separated from the others and must be examined together with them. Firstspace (physical space) is also always Secondspace (conceptualized space) and Thirdspace (lived space). When one looks out over a natural (physical) landscape, one does so through a conceptual spatial lens, and one experiences that landscape as lived space. Likewise, one's experience of space (as lived space) is an experience of a conceptualized physical space. In approaching lived space in this way, Soja seeks to move beyond the binary logic of either/or into a trialectical logic of both/and.

A simple example may help clarify Soja's theoretical spatial distinctions vis-à-vis Lefebvre. Consider the space you are occupying as you read this text. The physical space – dimensions of a room, furniture, window placement, temperature, etc. – is perceived space, the space presented to you through your five senses, Firstspace. This same space as conceived space, Secondspace, would be a photograph or architectural drawing of the space, or your mental picture of what the space will look like after renovation. Thirdspace – a synthesis of these two – addresses how one may experience space. The room you occupy might produce any number of possible responses: a sense of tranquility or oppression; fond memories or unpleasant ones. The point here is that space is never neutral, or merely a physical location that can be represented conceptually through a photograph, painting, architectural drawing, or map, as if the representation was a one-to-one likeness of the physical space.

	Lefebvre's terms	*Meaning*
Physical space	• perceived space • spatial practice	• physical, material space
Mental space	• conceived space • representations of space	• concepts/ideas about space
Social space	• lived space • spaces of representation	• space as experienced (physically, emotionally, intellectually, ideologically, etc.)

Lefebvre's work on the social production of space has significant implications for performance studies. His tripartite view of space lends itself well to the analysis of performance spaces, not least because it applies equally to such conventional performance spaces as theatres and opera houses and the broader spectrum of sites performance studies considers. A theatre, for example, is at one level a physical space occupied and perceived by performers and spectators. It is both a social space of representation (the performance) and a space in which representations of space occur. Stage sets are literally representations of space, but any kind of cultural performance may be said to create its own virtual space, a space that the anthropologist Victor Turner might describe as "liminal" or "subjunctive," simultaneously both perceptual and conceptual, both real and imagined. The geographical placement of a performance space, whether devoted to aesthetic, ritual, ceremonial, or any other kind of performance, in its social milieu (e.g. in the center of the community or at its margins) speaks to the status in that particular social world of the function to which that space is consecrated.

It is therefore unsurprising to find that Lefebvre's work on space has become a more or less obligatory point of reference for scholars whose work on performance foregrounds its spatial aspects. While some focus on developing analytical vocabularies and methods for the spatial analysis of performance, others take the spatial dimensions of performance in a particular social and historical setting as their subject, while still others explore the potential for rewriting the history of performance in terms of the way space has been used.

Further reading

By Lefebvre
Critique of Everyday Life, Volume 1. Translated by John Moore. London: Verso, 1991.
Critique of Everyday Life, Volume 2. Translated by John Moore. London: Verso, 2002.
Critique of Everyday Life, Volume 3: From Modernity to Modernism (Towards a Metaphilosophy of Daily Life). Translated by Gregory Elliott. London: Verso, 2003.
Henri Lefebvre: Key Writings. Edited by Stuart Elden, Elizabeth Lebas, and Eleonore Kofman. New York: Continuum, 2003.
The Production of Space. Translated by Donald Nicholson-Smith. Oxford: Blackwell, 1991.

About Lefebvre
Harvey, David. *The Condition of Postmodernity: An Enquiry into the Origins of Cultural Change*. Cambridge, MA: Blackwell, 1989.
*McAuley, Gay. *Space in Performance: Making Meaning in the Theatre*. Ann Arbor, MI: University of Michigan Press, 2000.

Mason, Jeffrey D. "Street Fairs: Social Space, Social Perfo
48, no. 3 (1996): 301–19.

Read, Alan. *Theatre and Everyday Life*. London: Routle

*Soja, Edward W. *Thirdspace: Journeys to Los A1
Imagined Places*. Malden, MA: Blackwell, 1996.

*Wiles, David. *A Short History of Western Per
Cambridge University Press, 2003.

22 E

Emmanuel Levinas

Key concepts

- ethics as first philosophy
- the Other (alterity)
- face-to-face
- transcendence

Emmanuel Levinas (1906–95) was born in Kovno, Lithuania. His parents were devout Jews and part of a distinguished Jewish community. In 1923 he moved to Strasbourg where he studied philosophy. In 1928–29 he studied under the phenomenologist Edmund Husserl in Freiburg. Soon after, he discovered the work of Heidegger, whom he would later criticize for his complicity with Nazism. In 1939 he began serving as a translator of German and Russian in the French military but was captured a year later by the Nazis who, on account of his officer's uniform, put him in a prisoner of war camp rather than a concentration camp. He described his life as dominated by the memory of Nazi horror. After the war, he studied Hebrew Scriptures and Talmud in Paris with the famous Monsieur Chouchani (who was then also teaching the young Holocaust survivor Elie Wiesel, another Lithuanian). In addition to his philosophical works, he wrote a number of important essays on Talmud.

Levinas served as teacher in and director of the Alliance Israelite Universelle until 1961, when he published his doctoral thesis, *Totality and Infinity*, and was appointed professor of philosophy at Poitiers. In 1967 he moved to the University of Paris-Nanterre, and in 1973 he took a position at the Sorbonne (Paris IV), from which he retired in 1976.

For most of Levinas's career he remained a relatively obscure philosopher, known primarily for his interpretations of Husserl and Heidegger (his early work on Husserl influenced Jean-Paul Sartre and Simone de Beauvoir, among others). Attention was drawn to Levinas's work in 1964 by Jacques DERRIDA's famous essay, called "Violence and Metaphysics," on *Totality and Infinity*. Since then his influence in the areas of philosophy, religious studies, and literary theory has grown exponentially. Levinas died on December 25, 1995 – the eighth day of Hanukkah that year.

Central to Levinas's philosophy is the claim that ethics – encapsulated in one's responsibility for and obligation to the Other – is the foundation of all philosophy and the heart of human existence. This is what he means in *Totality and Infinity* by **ethics as first philosophy**. The Oracle at Delphi gave us the philosophical dictum, "know yourself." But Levinas counters that the heart of philosophy is not about knowing and not about oneself alone. The heart of philosophy – the heart of life – is found not in knowing yourself but in your relation to **the Other**. The Other is essentially the not-me, that which is beyond me, exterior to me, outside the reach of my own system of thought, beyond my own self-understanding and understanding of the world.

In Levinas's writing, the privileged image for one's encounter with the Other is the **face-to-face**. The face of the Other confronts me in a non-symmetrical relationship. I am obliged to this Other, who implores, "do not kill me." Killing here should be taken both literally and figuratively. For one can kill, in Levinas's sense, simply by denying the Other's existence or by reducing the Other's otherness to oneself, that is, to sameness. When I "make sense" of the Other according to my own system of thought, when I explain the Other away, or when I regard the Other as a means to my own ends, I have killed the Other's otherness.

For Levinas, then, the face-to-face encounter is an "ultimate situation," for it is "present in its refusal to be contained" (*Totality and Infinity*, pp. 81 and 194). It obliges me to open myself to it, thereby breaking open my own self-contained identity and my own sense of security and at-homeness. The difficulty of doing this is enormous, for it requires me to extricate myself from the influence of deeply engrained social categories and styles of thought. For example, Julie Salverson ("Transgressive Storytelling") tells the story of an attempt in which she participated to create a video that would help ease tensions between Canadians and refugees in Canada by promoting openness to the other. The project failed, in Salverson's view, in part because the video did not enable the Canadian viewers to get past their desire to see themselves represented in it and their desire to empathize with the refugees. This kind of empathy is, in Levinas's terms, merely a mechanism of translating the Other into a version of ourselves, thus denying the Other's radical **alterity**.

For Levinas, the ultimate situation of the face-to-face encounter implies a kind of religious experience, that is, an encounter with **transcendence**, albeit not the kind of religious experience that tends to affirm or shore up the foundations of any religious certainty. Moreover, in one's relation to the individual other person (*Autrui*) in such an encounter, one becomes aware of radical, transcendent otherness, the wholly other (*autre*) or alterity, which cannot be contained in thought or reduced to a system and is ultimately beyond knowing. In this respect Levinas describes the individual face of the other as the trace of God. Thus, an encounter with the other person in a relationship of obligation is in the same moment an encounter with transcendence as exteriority, radical otherness. This encounter does not take place in a social vacuum – it is not a matter of a two-party, reciprocal relationship in which each participant plays the Other to the other one. Levinas also posits the presence of a third party to the face-to-face encounter who "looks at me in the eyes of the Other" (*Totality and Infinity*, p. 213) to remind me that even if I feel I have achieved a meaningful connection with an Other, there are always still others to whom I am an Other.

Levinas has not been nearly as influential in performance studies as in philosophy or literary criticism. Although his emphasis on face-to-face interaction between the self and the other would seem to constitute a useful framework for considering the ethical dimensions of performance, which is generally made up of encounters between performers and spectators, it is difficult to get past the question of whether spectatorship inevitably entails the objectification of the Other in terms determined by the self (the issue on which Salverson's project ran aground). Levinas himself points to this issue when he says: "There is something wicked and egoist and cowardly in artistic enjoyment. There are times when one can be ashamed of it, as of feasting during a plague" (*Collected Philosophical Papers*, p. 12). To the extent that the production of art or performance (which is not necessarily aesthetic in nature) entails representation of the other or the gratification of the self, it faces major obstacles to being considered ethical in Levinas's terms. Nevertheless, Levinas's philosophical framework is a valuable heuristic both for evaluating the ethicality of representations of the Other in specific cultural performances and for thinking through the issues inherent in an ethics of performance that would look past the content of specific performances to the relationships among human beings that underlie performance itself, as Jon Erickson demonstrates in "The Face and the Possibility of an Ethics of Performance."

Further reading

By Levinas

Collected Philosophical Papers. Translated by Alphonso Lingis. The Hague: Martinus Nijhoff, 1987.

Ethics and Infinity: Conversations with Philippe Nemo. Translated by Richard A. Cohen. Pittsburgh, PA: Duquesne University Press, 1985.

Is It Righteous to Be? Interviews with Emmanuel Levinas. Edited by Jill Robbins. Stanford, CA: Stanford University Press, 2001.

The Levinas Reader. Edited by Sean Hand. Oxford: Blackwell, 1990.

Totality and Infinity: An Essay on Exteriority. Translated by Alphonso Lingis. Pittsburgh, PA: Duquesne University Press, 1969.

About Levinas

Abrams, Joshua. "Ethics of the Witness: The Participatory Dances of Cie Felix Ruckert." In *Audience Participation: Essays on Inclusion in Performance*. Edited by Susan Kattwinkel. Westport, CT: Praeger, 2003.

Atterton, Peter. "Emmanuel Levinas." In *Postmodernism: The Key Figures*. Edited by Hans Bertens and Joseph Natoli. Oxford: Blackwell, 2002.

*Cornell, Drucilla. *The Philosophy of the Limit*. New York: Routledge, 1992.

Derrida, Jacques. *Adieu to Emmanuel Levinas*. Translated by Pascale-Anne Brault and Michael Naas. Stanford, CA: Stanford University Press, 1999.

Derrida, Jacques. "Violence and Metaphysics: An Essay on the Thought of Emmanuel Levinas." In *Writing and Difference*. Translated by Alan Bass. Chicago, IL: University of Chicago Press, 1978.

*Erickson, Jon. "The Face and the Possibility of an Ethics of Performance." *Journal of Dramatic Theory and Criticism* 13, no. 2 (1999): 5–21.

Nealon, Jeffrey T. "The Ethics of Dialogue: Bakhtin and Levinas." *College English* 59, no. 2 (1997): 129–48.

Pugliese, Joseph. "Penal Asylum: Refugees, Ethics, Hospitality." *borderlands e-journal* 1, no. 1 (2002). Online, available at: www.borderlandsejournal.adelaide. edu.au/vol1no1_2002/pugliese.html

Salverson, Julie. "Transgressive Storytelling or an Aesthetic of Injury: Performance, Pedagogy and Ethics." *Theatre Research in Canada* 20, no. 1 (1999): 35–51.

23 Jean-François Lyotard

Key concepts

- metanarrative
- postmodern condition
- language game
- performativity
- *petits récits*
- differend

Jean-François Lyotard (1924–98) was born in Versailles, France and studied phenomenology under Maurice MERLEAU-PONTY. He began his career as a secondary school teacher in Algeria, and later taught philosophy at the University of Paris, from which he retired in 1989. He then went on to visiting professorships at several American universities, including Yale and Emory. He died of leukemia in Paris in 1998.

From his earliest work, Lyotard displayed resistance to the so-called structuralist "linguistic turn" which emphasized the way language shapes experience and which was so influential among many of his contemporaries in France in the 1950s and 1960s (e.g. Lévi-Strauss, LACAN, BARTHES). He insisted that there is always a chasm between experience and language, and that one must not rule out extra-linguistic experience. Language, he insisted, does not construct our lifeworld completely; there are experiences that language does not and cannot present. In the essay "The Tooth, the Palm" (published in French in 1973), Lyotard used the theatre as a context for discussing the inadequacy of the linguistic model to account for contemporary society. Under advanced capitalism, "everything is exchangeable, reciprocally" and it is no longer possible to distinguish signifiers from signifieds: anything can assume either position in relation to anything else ("The Tooth, the Palm," p. 26). He called, therefore, for a theatre that would operate beyond the logic of the sign whose purpose would not be to "suggest that such and such means such and such" but to "produce the highest intensity . . . of what there is, without intention" ("The Tooth, the Palm," p. 31).

Lyotard's two most influential works are *The Postmodern Condition* (1979), originally written as a report on the current state of knowledge for the government of Quebec, and *The Differend* (1983). The two are closely related and together provide a valuable introduction to Lyotard's philosophy.

A key concept in *The Postmodern Condition* is **metanarrative** or "master narrative." Lyotard uses this term to refer to the overarching mythic narratives which individuals and societies tell in order to situate their particular time and place within the context of a larger story, thereby giving it broader significance. A metanarrative locates a current situation, whether individual or communal, within a larger narrative structure that plots movement toward some ultimate objective – progress, triumph of reason, victory of the proletariat, redemption.

The **postmodern condition** – ascribed to the contemporary west – is one in which there is an increasing "incredulity" and distrust toward metanarratives. In place of a world governed by metanarratives, Lyotard envisages a postmodern world made up of multiple, incommensurable **language games** (a concept he borrowed from the German philosopher Ludwig Wittgenstein) in which different groups literally cannot speak to one another. One characteristic of the postmodern condition is therefore a crisis of legitimation. Since no discourse can legitimize itself by reference to metanarratives and no discourse can legitimize another discourse, discourses have to find other means of legitimation. Since science and education, for instance, no longer can legitimize themselves by claiming to improve people's lives, they do so by reference to the concept of technological **performativity**. For Lyotard, performativity means something quite different than it does for J.L. Austin and, consequently, for Judith BUTLER. Far from being a linguistic function, Lyotard's performativity is a quantifiable measure of efficiency: "the principle of optimal performance maximizing output . . . and minimizing input" (*The Postmodern Condition*, p. 44). For Lyotard, performativity in this sense has become the dominant form of legitimation in postmodern society. In this context, information is power: the more information one has, the greater performativity one can achieve. As more and more information is gathered in digital form and stored in databases, the questions of who owns those databases and who has access to them become ever more urgent.

Lyotard argues that metanarratives are being replaced by a proliferation of *petits récits*, "little stories" or testimonies that draw attention to particulars as opposed to universals – that is, to local events, individual experiences, heterodox ideas, and other practices and narratives that do not fit within a larger, universal metanarrative. Within the postmodern condition there is a new found interest in the particular differences and dissensions that challenge the drive toward homogeneity and oneness, a drive which is propelled by a totalizing metanarrative that Lyotard describes as "totalitarian." Against this drive, Lyotard urges us to "wage war on totality; let us be witness to the unpresentable; let us activate the differences and save the honor of the name" (*The Postmodern Condition*, p. 82).

Lyotard continues this line of thought, including its ethical imperative to activate particular differences against totalizing universals, in *The Differend*. Here, Lyotard uses the term **differend** to explain the silencing of particular differences that do not fit within larger conceptual or social totalities. It is the sign that someone or something has been denied voice or visibility because it has been viewed by the dominant ideological system as unacceptable. Such radical differences are suppressed because they cannot be subsumed under larger, "universal" concepts without doing violence to them. "Differend" means at once dispute, difference, and otherness (alterity).

In both its choices of objects and analytical methods, performance studies often reflects Lyotard's emphasis of *petits récits*, challenging totality, and respecting difference. Although "postmodern performance" has become a trope in performance studies, Lyotard's concept of postmodernism as the age of legitimation through performativity has not had as much direct impact on performance studies as that of other theorists of postmodernity, though it has important implications. For one thing, the question of how relationships between audiences and performances are to be understood takes on a new urgency in light of the atomization of postmodern society. If every social grouping has its own language game, what kinds of interactions and communication are possible or even desirable in performance? Lyotard's ideas concerning the importance of the computerization of society and information as power are a good matrix for thinking about the use of digital technologies in performance. And, as Jon McKenzie has pointed out in *Perform or Else*, Lyotard makes it clear that performance is not necessarily counter-hegemonic, as performance studies so often assumes: in the form of performativity, performance sustains the power of the status quo rather than challenging it.

Further reading

By Lyotard

*The Differend: Phrases in Dispute. Translated by Georges Van Den Abbeele. Minneapolis, MN: University of Minnesota Press, 1989.

*The Postmodern Condition: A Report on Knowledge. Translated by Geoff Bennington and Brian Massumi. Minneapolis, MN: University of Minnesota Press, 1984.

The Postmodern Explained to Children: Correspondence, 1982–1985. Translated by Don Barry et al. London: Turnaround, 1992.

"The Tooth, the Palm." Translated by Anne Knap and Michel Benamou. In Performance, Vol. II. Edited by Philip Auslander. London: Routledge, 2003. Originally published in Sub-Stance 15 (1976): 105–10.

About Lyotard

Birringer, Johannes. "Overexposure: Les Immatériaux." Performing Arts Journal 10, no. 2 (1986): 6–11.

Brewer, Mária Minich. "Performing Theory." *Theatre Journal* 37, no. 1 (1985): 12–30.

Broadhurst, Sue. "Liminal Aesthetics." *Body, Space and Technology Journal* 1, no. 1 (2000). Online, available at: http://people.brunel.ac.uk / bst / 1no1 / journal.htm

Brügger, Niels. "What about the Postmodern? The Concept of the Postmodern in the Work of Lyotard." *Yale French Studies* 99 (2001): 77–92.

McKenzie, Jon. *Perform or Else: From Discipline to Performance*. London: Routledge, 2001.

Rayner, Alice. "The Audience: Subjectivity, Community and the Ethics of Listening." In *Performance: Critical Concepts*, Vol. II. Edited by Philip Auslander. London: Routledge, 2003. Originally published in *Journal of Dramatic Theory and Criticism* 7 (1993): 3–24.

Ridout, Nicholas. "Lyotard on Theatre: Last 'Blow-Back'." In *Stage Fright, Animals, and Other Theatrical Problems*. Cambridge: Cambridge University Press, 2006.

24 Maurice Merleau-Ponty

Key concepts

- primacy of perception
- lived experience
- lived body
- embodiment
- body-subject

Maurice Merleau-Ponty (1908–61) was a French intellectual particularly interested in the nature of human consciousness as embodied experience. He was born in Rochefort-sur-mer, France. As a student at the École normale supérieure, he became interested in phenomenology – the philosophical study of the perception of things – through the work of Husserl and Heidegger. After graduating in 1930, Merleau-Ponty taught at different high schools. During the 1930s he was associated with the leftist Catholic journal, *Esprit*.

Merleau-Ponty served as an officer in the French army at the beginning of World War II. During the German occupation, while participating in the French Resistance, he taught in Paris and composed *The Phenomenology of Perception* (published in French in 1945), widely regarded as his most important work. Following the war, he co-founded the existentialist journal, *Les Temps modernes*, along with Jean-Paul Sartre and Simone de Beauvoir. In 1952, after repeated political disagreements with Sartre over the latter's support of North Korea during the Korean War, Merleau-Ponty resigned from the journal's editorial board. Merleau-Ponty's post-war academic career included academic positions at the Sorbonne and, from 1952 until his death, at the Collège de France.

Merleau-Ponty's thought centers on understanding the lived, embodied nature of human consciousness and perception. Among noted theorists influenced by Merleau-Ponty's work were Claude Lévi-Strauss, Michel FOUCAULT, Paul Ricoeur, and Louis ALTHUSSER. More recently, Merleau-Ponty's work has been pursued by social scientists interested in critiquing traditional assumptions about the relationship between body and mind, and the nature of human experience. In order to understand Merleau-Ponty's philosophical views, we need to briefly consider phenomenology, a perspective that informs much of his thinking. As the name suggests, phenomenology explores phenomena – anything perceived directly by the senses. The German founder of phenomenology, Edmund Husserl, argues that although philosophical proofs for the independent existence of objects perceived through the senses are impossibly difficult to establish, human beings nevertheless experience the external world as objects of consciousness, regardless of the ultimate ontological status of these things. Husserl says that we need to "bracket off" concern over proofs and other questions for which definitive answers are not readily forthcoming. Instead, he says, we should concentrate on investigating the sensual perceptions that constitute our experiences of ideas, images, emotions, objects, and other things that are perceived through consciousness. The main concern, however, is with the experience of these objects that engage our attention, not with an analysis of their status independent of our consciousness. Thus, Husserl established phenomenology as the analysis of experiences that result from consciousness of external objects.

Merleau-Ponty's intellectual contributions are, in part, extensions of Husserl's version of phenomenology and center on the concepts of embodiment and perception. These ideas are explored in *The Phenomenology of Perception*. Here Merleau-Ponty critiques the Cartesian body/mind dichotomy by arguing for the collapse of this dualistic way of understanding human beings existing in the world. He emphasizes the necessity to recognize that people are not simply – or primarily – disembodied thinking minds, but rather bodies connected to a material world. Bodies are, therefore, not something abstract, but rather concrete entities in the world through which perception occurs and subjectivity is formed. For Merleau-Ponty, the world is the ground of experience. Any subjectivity is of the world, not separate or disconnected from it, and is fueled by what he terms the **primacy of perception**. Our access to the world is through the body not through, or only through, the mind. Contrary to Descartes' dictum, *Cogito ergo sum* ("I think, therefore I am"), existence is not thinking but embodiment. Indeed, all thinking is embodied; it derives from consciousness which itself develops from the subject's bodily perceptions. These perceptions undergird rationalization and other conscious and logical operations on their meaning.

In the Husserlian view (itself indebted to Cartesian philosophy), human beings are entities centered on consciousness. Against this view, Merleau-Ponty insists that human identity – our subjectivity – is informed significantly by our physicality, our bodies. He therefore asserts the centrality of the body and the body's influence on our perception of the experienced world. Knowledge of the world, he says, derives from concrete perception, not from abstract thought or the workings of a disembodied mind or consciousness. In short, he prioritizes the body over the mind in our experience of the world. Perception itself is incarnate: perceptions do not exist as bodiless abstractions but rather within bodies. Perception occurs only in the world of lived experience. Perception does not exist as an abstraction transcending or standing outside of the lived body.

Merleau-Ponty asserted that it is through **lived experience** that we gain knowledge of the world. He states that the activities of the body in the world constitute lived experience. Such experience is never fixed, but is always in process. We both shape and are shaped by our lived experiences. The mind that perceives things is incarnate in the body. Perception and consciousness are not separate from or transcendent of lived experience in the world.

Perception is directly connected to the **lived body**. By lived body, Merleau-Ponty is referring to both the body that experiences the world and the body that is experienced. The subject (person) doing the perceiving is embodied. This embodiment is thus the link to the external, phenomenal, experienced world. Humans consist of conscious components, but it is our bodily aspects that determine who we are. Despite the insistence by some influential philosophers that consciousness is foundational to what it means to be a human being, Merleau-Ponty argues that whatever we experience in the world or understand about the world derives fundamentally from our bodies and our embodied minds. Perception underpins categorization or theorization even if it appears that we have thoughts and conceptualizations about the world that we only secondarily experience physically. The world can be viewed only from our physical time and place. As Merleau-Ponty states: "Our own body is in the world as the heart is in the organism: it keeps the visible spectacle constantly alive, it breathes life into it and sustains it inwardly, and with it forms a system" (*The Phenomenology of Perception*, p. 235).

A key idea expressed in Merleau-Ponty's work is the notion of **embodiment**. According to Merleau-Ponty, it is not just the mind which perceives, experiences, and represents the world – a traditional philosophical view of the centrality of mind. Instead, the concept of embodiment asserts that the body plays a central role in how one experiences the world. As Merleau-Ponty understands it, the world is not an external object to think about, but rather is the ground for our perceptions and experiences. Thus, the external things we perceive as objects in the world are the result of how our bodies experience them, not simply the product of consciousness recognizing the object. Philosophical ideas that consciousness does all the work of perceiving the world are erroneous. From Merleau-Ponty's perspective, you cannot have consciousness without the body – body and mind are inextricably bound. Subjectivity, then, is incarnate. For Merleau-Ponty, embodied knowledge precludes the possibility of a realm of autonomous knowledge gained prior to or without the body. Analysis of the world is always the activity of an embodied mind.

The concept of **body-subject** is used by Merleau-Ponty in *The Phenomenology of Perception* to refer to the idea that the body, mind, and world are completely intertwined and not separable as Cartesian thought asserts. Merleau-Ponty's phenomenology seeks to understand this interconnection, not to try to locate some immutable consciousness transcending the world as experienced by bodies. The notion of body-subject underscores Merleau-Ponty's insistence that it is a body that connects a person to the world. Cartesian duality breaks down at this juncture. There is no disembodied mind that observes objects out there in the world. We live in the world by way of our bodies. Subject and object are a unity, not a duality. That is, you must not treat them as separate realms, but rather as two sides of the same entity that exists – embodied – in the world.

Phenomenology was one of several theoretical and philosophical approaches with which performance scholars began to engage in the mid-1980s. It was somewhat overshadowed by various structuralist and poststructuralist frameworks, including semiotics and deconstruction, in which the body is understood more as a socially constructed or encoded text than as the locus of primary, prediscursive experience. Nevertheless, Merleau-Ponty's body-centric way of thinking proved appealing to scholars of theatre, dance, and performance art precisely because these forms often foreground the expressive body, and phenomenology provides a vocabulary for talking about experiential aspects of performance that are otherwise difficult to encapsulate. Some writers, notably Bert States and Stanton Garner, sought theoretical rapprochements between phenomenology and semiotics or deconstruction, feeling that combinations of these approaches could produce useful lenses for understanding and analyzing theatre and drama. Merleau-Ponty's concept of embodiment speaks potentially to all aspects of performance: the performer's embodied experience of performing as much as the spectator's embodied perception of the performance; it can also provide insight into the phenomenal presence of objects in performance and methods of training performers.

Further reading

By Merleau-Ponty

The Essential Writings of Merleau-Ponty. Edited by Alden L. Fisher. New York: Harcourt, Brace and World, 1969.

**The Phenomenology of Perception*, 2nd edn. Translated by Colin Smith. London: Routledge, 2002.

The Primacy of Perception. Translated by James M. Edie. Evanston, IL: Northwestern University Press, 1964.

The Structure of Behavior. Translated by Alden L. Fisher. Boston, MA: Beacon Press, 1963.

The Visible and the Invisible. Edited by Claude Lefort. Translated by Alphonso Lingis. Evanston, IL: Northwestern University Press, 1968.

About Merleau-Ponty

Connolly, Maureen and Lathrop, Anna. "Maurice Merleau-Ponty and Rudolf Laban – An Interactive Appropriation of Parallels and Resonances." *Human Studies* 20, no. 1 (1997): 27–45.

Dillon, M.C. *Merleau-Ponty's Ontology*, 2nd edn. Evanston, IL: Northwestern University Press, 1997.

Evans, Fred, and Lawlor, Leonard (eds). *Chiasms: Merleau-Ponty's Notion of Flesh*. Albany, NY: State University of New York Press, 2000.

Fraleigh, Sondra. "A Vulnerable Glance: Seeing Dance through Phenomenology." *Dance Research Journal* 23, no. 1 (1991): 11–16.

* Garner, Stanton. *Bodied Spaces: Phenomenology and Performance in Contemporary Drama*. Ithaca, NY: Cornell University Press, 1994.

Jones, Amelia. *Body Art / Performing the Subject*. Minneapolis, MN: University of Minnesota Press, 1998.

Langer, Monika M. *Merleau-Ponty's Phenomenology of Perception: A Guide and Commentary*. Tallahassee, FL: Florida State University Press, 1989.

* Priest, Stephen. *Merleau-Ponty*. London: Routledge, 1998.

Primozic, Daniel Thomas. *On Merleau-Ponty*. Belmont, CA: Wadsworth, 2001.

Rayner, Alice. *To Act To Do To Perform: Drama and the Phenomenology of Action*. Ann Arbor, MI: University of Michigan Press, 1994.

Smith, Mary Lynn. "Moving Self: The Thread which Bridges Dance and Theatre." *Research in Dance Education* 3, no. 2 (2002): 123–41.

States, Bert O. *Great Reckonings in Little Rooms: On Phenomenology of Theater*. Ithaca, NY: Cornell University Press, 1971.

States, Bert O. "The Phenomenological Attitude." In *Critical Theory and Performance*. Edited by Janelle Reinelt and Joseph Roach. Ann Arbor, MI: University of Michigan Press, 1992.

Zarrilli, Phillip B. "Toward a Phenomenological Model of the Actor's Embodied Modes of Experience." *Theatre Journal* 56 (2004): 653–66.

25 Edward W. Said

Key concepts

- postcolonial criticism
- colonial discourse
- Orientalism
- imperialism
- contrapuntal reading

Edward W. Said (1935–2003) was a postcolonial literary critic and the Parr Professor of English and Comparative Literature at Columbia University. Born in Jerusalem, Said's Palestinian family became refugees in 1948 and moved to Egypt, where he attended British schools. He also spent time during his youth in Lebanon and Jordan before immigrating to the United States. He earned his BA from Princeton University in 1957 and his PhD in literature from Harvard University in 1964. While at Princeton, he also studied piano at the Juilliard School in New York. He spent his entire academic career as Professor of English and Comparative Literature at Columbia University. He died in New York in 2003 after a long battle with leukemia.

Said's work included both intellectual and political pursuits. On the one hand, he is well known for his engagements with literary criticism and post-colonial theory, often drawing from theoretical perspectives and methods developed by Michel FOUCAULT. On the other hand, he was politically active as an advocate of Palestinian independence and human rights. Critical of US foreign policy, especially in the Middle East, he also spoke out against corruption within Palestine.

Said's intellectual and political agendas address the ways in which white Europeans and North Americans fail to understand – or even try to under-stand – differences between western culture and non-western cultures. His studies on Orientalism expressly address this complex of issues. This work has arguably the deepest resonance for performance studies, especially for those dealing with non-western performance or for the representation of the East in western performance.

Said's **postcolonial criticism** is particularly concerned with issues of discourse and representation in relation to the history of western colo-nialism. Said asks questions about how colonized cultures are represented, about the power of these representations to shape and control other cultures, and about **colonial discourse**, that is, the discourse through which colonizer/colonized subject positions are constructed.

Following Foucault, Said understands discourse as systems of linguistic usage and codes – discursive formations, whether written or spoken – that produce knowledge and practice about particular conceptual fields, demarcating what can be known, said, or enacted in relation to this body of knowledge. Thus, for example, medical discourse establishes knowledge about such things as the hierarchical nature of the doctor–patient relationship, the identification and classification of diseases, and distinctions between physical and mental illness. It is through different discourses that we know about and categorize the world. For Foucault, there are significant ramifications to the discursive process. In any cultural setting, there are dominant groups that establish what can and cannot be said and done by others on the basis of the discursive knowledge they impose on others – the dominated. In the end, both dominant and dominated are made into subjects of this knowledge and live within the parameters that the discursive knowledge allows. This knowledge attains the status or appearance of an independent reality, and its origins as a social construction are forgotten. Discursive knowledge is also invariably connected to power. Those in control of a particular discourse have control over what can be known and hence power over others.

Discourse, as a form of knowledge that exerts power, is of particular importance in Said's articulation of the nature of **Orientalism**, western discourse about the East that engenders the oppressor–oppressed relationship pertaining between colonizer and colonized: see especially Said's *Orientalism* (1978) and *Culture and Imperialism* (1993). Said focuses on the ways in which discursive formations about the "Orient" exert power and control over those subjected to them. For Said, the concept of Orientalism has three dimensions: the discursive, the academic, and the imaginative. All three, though, are interconnected and should be understood as such. The *discursive* concerns the notion that

> Orientalism can be discussed and analyzed as the corporate institution for dealing with the Orient – dealing with it by making statements about it, authorizing views of it, describing it, by teaching it, settling it, ruling over it: in short, Orientalism as a Western style for dominating, restructuring, and having authority over the Orient.
>
> (*Orientalism*, p. 3)

The *academic* refers to:

> Anyone who teaches, writes about, or researches the Orient – and this applies whether the person is an anthropologist, sociologist, historian, or philologist – either in its specific or its general aspects, is an Orientalist, and what he or she does is Orientalism.
>
> (*Orientalism*, p. 2)

Finally, the *imaginative* refers to the idea that "Orientalism is a style of thought based upon an ontological and epistemological distinction made between 'the Orient' and (most of the time) 'the Occident'" (*Orientalism*, p. 2). Said refers to this culturally constructed space as an "imaginative geography" (*Orientalism*, p. 54).

Orientalism, Said's groundbreaking study which explores the intellectual history of European (particularly British and French) representations of the Arab Middle East, is an early example of postcolonial criticism. Indeed, Said's work on Orientalism cannot be understood without framing it within the larger concept of postcolonialism and the postcolonial theory that examines it. Postcolonial theory and criticism, which became prominent in the 1990s, is concerned with analyzing the relationship between culture and colonial power, exploring the cultural products of societies that were once under colonial rule. Postcolonial Indian and African literature, for instance, addresses such issues as the lingering effects of colonialism on identity, nationality, and the nature of resistance to colonial power.

One goal of postcolonial theory is to question universal, humanist claims that cultural products can contain timeless and culturally transcendent ideas and values. When, for instance, colonizing nations make universal claims – claiming to make judgments on the basis of some universal standard – the colonized, other culture is by default seen as tentative and provisional. These other cultures are somehow "less than" the colonial power. Victorian British literature often claims to represent the universal human condition. In so doing, Indian culture is seen – whether consciously or unconsciously – as misrepresenting the truth or reality discoverable in the world by those with the ability to do so. Postcolonial theory refutes this universalist impulse and instead seeks to give voice to local practices, ideas, and values. Eurocentrism, which places Europe at the center and relegates non-European culture to the margins, is seen as a hegemonic power that must be resisted. A problematic side-effect of colonialism is that in a postcolonial culture a people have to locate strategies for reclaiming their cultural past and prizing its value.

The nature of colonial discourse and the ways in which it was used to wield power and control over the colonized is therefore central to Said's thesis in *Orientalism*. This volume explicates ways in which western colonizers constructed the colonized as "other." Ways in which colonizers represented the colonized also created a social hierarchy and hegemonic power over the colonized. Said's analysis focuses especially on the Middle East as "Orient," but his thesis can be extended to other cultural contexts where colonization occurred (and is still occurring).

Said critiques Eurocentric universalism for its setting up a binary opposition of the superiority of western cultures and the inferiority of colonized, non-western cultures. Said identifies this perspective as a central aspect of Orientalism. This view sees the Middle East – and by extension – Africa, South and Southeast Asia, and East Asia – as the "Orient," an "other" inferior to western culture. Said points out that Orientalist discourse has the pernicious effect of treating the colonized as if they were all the same. Thus,

"Orientals" are perceived not as freely choosing, autonomous individuals, but rather as homogeneous, faceless peoples who are known by their commonality of values, emotions, and personality traits. They are, in effect, essentialized to a few stereotypical – and often negative – characteristics and rendered as lacking individual personalities. A strong racist tendency is also operating in such views. Said provides numerous accounts of colonial administrators and travelers who describe and represent Arabs in dehumanizing ways. After citing one such example he remarks: "In such statements as these, we note immediately that 'the Arab' or 'Arabs' have an aura of apartness, definiteness, and collective self-consistency such as to wipe out any traces of individual Arabs with narratable life histories" (*Orientalism*, p. 229).

Orientalist discourse, says Said, makes possible "the enormous systematic discipline by which European culture was able to manage – and even produce – the Orient politically, sociologically, militarily, ideologically, scientifically, and imaginatively during the post-Enlightenment period" (*Orientalism*, p. 3). Said is less interested in refuting some notion that this discourse is "true" in some essential, transcendent way than with marking out the ground by which colonial discourse acted on the objects of its knowledge claims. Said asserts that, "The Orient was almost a European invention, and had been since antiquity a place of romance, exotic beings, haunting memories and landscapes, remarkable experiences" (*Orientalism*, p. 1). For Said, the issue is not whether this European representation is true, but rather its effects in the world.

If colonial discourse oppressed the colonized subject, it also worked its effects on those who wielded this language in the first place. For Said, Orientalism delineates a relationship between "Europe" and the "Orient." For instance, the concept of "the Orient has helped to define Europe (or the West) as its contrasting image, idea, personality, experience" (*Orientalism*, pp. 1–2). Thus, European identity is framed in terms of what it is or – more likely – is not in relation to a constructed "Orient." Concepts of the Orient also create a self-identity for Europe. "Europe" is as much a fiction as is the Orient if by "Europe" we mean some homogenous entity that is known by a set of essential "European" characteristics.

In a later study, *Culture and Imperialism*, Said draws a distinction between **imperialism** and colonialism. For Said, "'imperialism' means the practice, the theory, and the attitudes of a dominating metropolitan center ruling a distant territory; 'colonialism,' which is almost always a consequence of imperialism, is the implanting of settlements on distant territory" (*Culture and Imperialism*, p. 9). Imperialism is embedded in colonial discourse and serves as an important tool for creating the colonized subject. Said argues that any discourse that comments on a colonized culture cannot remain neutral or stand outside of a consideration of imperialism, because all such discourses are invested in how the view of the other is constructed. One need only consult the literature, history, and other cultural products of a colonizing nation that are directed at the colonized to find, for instance, the colonized equated with the "other."

How might one tease out from a text those aspects of colonial discourse that may be embedded therein? Said's notion of **contrapuntal reading** is particularly suggestive. Borrowing the concept of counterpoint from music, Said describes a strategy for reading that exposes the colonial discourses hidden within a text. Contrapuntal reading not only unveils the colonial perspective, but also tries to read for nuances of resistance (counterpoints) that may also be lurking within the narrative. Said argues that we need to "read the great canonical texts, and perhaps the entire archive of modern and pre-modern European and American culture, with an effort to draw out, extend, give emphasis and voice to what is silent or marginally present or ideologically represented" (*Culture and Imperialism*, p. 66). In practice, says Said, reading contrapuntally "means reading a text with an understanding of what is involved when an author shows, for instance, that a colonial sugar plantation is seen as important to the process of maintaining a particular style of life in England" (*Culture and Imperialism*, p. 66).

Said's primary connection to performance was through music. An accomplished pianist himself, he regularly wrote on music and opera for *The Nation*. It is interesting that he focused almost exclusively on Western classical music, for which he advocated staunchly, though not uncritically. He examined the influence of Orientalist discourses on Verdi's *Aïda* in *Culture and Imperialism*, for example, and noted more generally both the ways in which music has been complicit with the authoritative forces in civil society and its more transgressive potential: "that faculty music has to travel, cross over, drift from place to place in a society, even though many institutions and orthodoxies sought to confine it" (*Musical Elaborations*, p. xix). In his work on music, Said combined critical analysis with social action, as he did in his other work. He formed a friendship with the Argentine-Israeli pianist and conductor Daniel Barenboim that led both to Barenboim's performing for a Palestinian audience on the West Bank and the formation of the West-Eastern Divan Workshop and Orchestra, devoted to bringing together promising young Israeli and Arab musicians to work together on neutral ground in Europe.

Said's book *Musical Elaborations* (1991), based on a series of lectures he gave in 1989, is his most sustained discussion of music. In the first chapter "Performance as an Extreme Occasion," Said offers some suggestive thoughts on the performance of classical music. He argues, first of all, that the conventions of musical performance should be analyzed as products of specific historical, cultural, sociological, political, and economic forces and conditions, much the way texts are analyzed in cultural studies. He discusses the way that classical music is now performed as an example of such analysis. Whereas in the past, musicians were also frequently composers or had a close relationship with those whose music they played, and the audience often entertained itself by performing similar music at home, classical music performance today has become a highly specialized and rarified activity focused entirely on the marketing of virtuosic performers. Concerts are therefore "extreme occasions" cut off from the rest of life. Said closely examines the work of two performers, the conductor Arturo Toscanini and the pianist Glenn Gould, to argue that each in his own way, through particular excesses and idiosyncracies, heightened the conventions of classical music performance to such a degree that their particularity and artificiality became overt. By so doing, they turned performance into metaperformance, a kind of sociological commentary on itself: "they elucidate and dramatize the fate of music and music-making as it gets concentrated and constricted into the performance occasion" (*Musical Elaborations*, p. 21).

Although Said is frequently cited by performance scholars working on Orientalism or postcolonialism, sustained engagement with his work is rare. Said's keen sense of the social and historical emplacement not just of texts but also of performance conventions, and the ways that performers can perform both texts and conventions "against the grain," perhaps by pushing them to extremes, are of considerable value to those engaged with performance.

Further reading

By Said

Culture and Imperialism. New York: Alfred A. Knopf, 1993.

*Musical Elaborations. New York: Columbia University Press, 1991.

"On Jean Genet's Late Works." In *Imperialism and Theatre: Essays on World Theatre, Drama and Performance*. Edited by J. Ellen Gainor. London: Routledge, 1995.

*Orientalism. New York: Pantheon, 1978.

The World, the Text, and the Critic. Cambridge, MA: Harvard University Press, 1983.

About Said

*Ashcroft, Bill, and Ahluwalia, Pal. *Edward Said*. London: Routledge, 2001.

Buse, Peter. "Culture and Colonies: Wertenbaker with Said." In *Drama + Theory: Critical Approaches to Modern British Drama*. Manchester: Manchester University Press, 2001.

Hammond, Clare. "The Relevance of Edward Said's Theory of Orientalism to Mozart's *Die Entführung aus dem Serail*." *British Postgraduate Musicology* 8 (2006). Online, available at: www.bpmonline.org.uk/bpm8/Hammond.html

Hays, Michael. "Representing Empire: Class, Culture, and the Popular Theatre in the Nineteenth Century." In *Imperialism and Theatre: Essays on World Theatre, Drama and Performance*. Edited by J. Ellen Gainor. London: Routledge, 1995.

Marranca, Bonnie. "Criticism, Culture and Performance: An Interview with Edward Said." *Performing Arts Journal* 13, no. 1 (1991): 21–42.

Miller, Dan. "Privacy and Pleasure: Edward Said on Music." *Postmodern Culture* 2, no. 1 (1991). Online, available at: http://muse.jhu.edu.proxy-remote.galib.uga.edu:2048/journals/postmodern_culture/v002/2.1r_miller.html

26 Gayatri Chakravorty Spivak

Key concepts

- the subaltern
- othering
- worlding
- strategic essentialism

Gayatri Chakravorty Spivak (1942–) is a Bengali cultural and literary critic. Born in Calcutta, India to a middle-class family during the waning years of British colonial rule, she attended Presidency College of the University of Calcutta, graduating in 1959 with a degree in English literature. She moved to the United States in 1962 and attended graduate school at Cornell University, where she received her PhD in comparative literature under the direction of Paul de Man, who introduced her to the work of Jacques DERRIDA. Her 1977 translation of Derrida's *Of Grammatology* (1967) into English made Derrida's work available to a wider audience. She gained initial notoriety from her outstanding introduction to that work, quickly becoming recognized among English-speaking academics seeking help in understanding Derrida's text. Spivak is currently Avalon Foundation Professor in the Humanities at Columbia University.

Spivak operates at the intersections of postcolonial theory, feminism, deconstruction, and Marxism. She rigorously interrogates the binary oppositions that animate both postcolonial and feminist discourse. She further questions concepts found in the imperialist language of colonizers, including concepts of nationhood, fixed identity, and the developing world. The numerous articles and interviews that comprise Spivak's scholarly production have been compiled into several books. *In Other Worlds: Essays in Cultural Politics* (1987) is a collection of essays on a wide range of topics, from Virginia Wolfe's *To the Lighthouse*, to French feminism, to the concept of "value." *The Post-Colonial Critic: Interviews, Strategies, Dialogues* (1990) is a compilation of interviews that present Spivak's often difficult thinking in a more reader-friendly format. *Outside in the Teaching Machine*

(1993) brings together Spivak's writings on higher education and globalization. *A Critique of Postcolonial Reason: Toward a History of the Vanishing Present* (1999) both expands on her studies of the postcolonial – she explores, for instance, the idea of the "native informant" – and reconsiders and revises some of her earlier work.

Fundamental to Spivak's work is the concept of **the subaltern**. Subaltern means "of inferior rank." Spivak borrows the term from Antonio Gramsci, who used it to refer to social groups under the hegemonic control of the ruling elite. In this sense, the term can refer to any group that is collectively subordinated or disenfranchised, whether on the basis of race, ethnicity, sex, religion, or any other category of identity. Spivak, however, uses this term specifically to refer to the colonized and peripheral subject, especially with reference to those oppressed by British colonialism, such as segments of the Indian population prior to independence. Spivak emphasizes the fact that the female subaltern subject is even more peripheral and marginalized than the male. In the essay, "Can the Subaltern Speak?" (1985), Spivak observes: "If in the context of colonial production, the subaltern has no history, and cannot speak, the subaltern as female is even more deeply in shadow" ("Can the Subaltern Speak?" p. 28). Spivak's notion of the subaltern is thus also implicated in feminist concerns. She discusses ways that colonialism – and its patriarchy – silences subaltern voices to the extent that they have no conceptual space from which they can speak and be heard, unless, perhaps, they assume the discourse of the oppressing colonizer. The original version of "Can the Subaltern Speak?" discussed here has been enormously influential in postcolonial theoretical circles. But I should note that Spivak has more recently revised aspects of her theory of the subaltern in her 1999 book, *A Critique of Postcolonial Reason: Toward a History of the Vanishing Present* (see especially pp. 306–11).

Another aspect of western colonialism explored by Spivak is the way that colonial discourse participates in a process she refers to as **othering**. Othering – a term derived from a whole corpus of texts by Hegel, LACAN, Sartre, and others – is an ideological process that isolates groups that are seen as different from the norm of the colonizers. For Spivak, othering is the way in which imperial discourse creates colonized, subaltern subjects. Like Edward SAID, she views othering dialectically: the colonizing subject is created in the same moment as the subaltern subject. In this sense, othering expresses a hierarchical, unequal relationship. In her research into this process, Spivak utilizes British colonial office dispatches to reveal othering in historical context. Yet she makes clear that othering is embedded in the discourse of various forms of colonial narrative, fiction as well as non-fiction.

In "Acting Bits/Identity Talk" (1992), Spivak uses a performance metaphor to describe the process of othering (though she does not use that word in this case):

What we call experience is the staging of experience. . . . A most tenacious name, as well as the strongest account of the agency or mechanics of the staging of "experience-in-identity" is "origin": "I perform my life this way because my origin stages me so." National origin, ethnic origin. And, more pernicious: "You cannot help acting this way because your origin stages you so."

("Acting Bits/Identity Talk," p. 781)

Spivak employs the theatrical metaphor to suggest both the subject's relative lack of agency with respect to her own identity (she is not fully in control of the way her identity is staged) and the subject's internalization of external characterizations as her own identity (a process related to ALTHUSSER'S concept of interpellation).

Spivak's concept of **worlding**, derived from Heidegger, is closely related to the dynamics of othering in colonial discourse. Worlding is the process whereby a colonized space is made present in and present to a world crafted by colonial discourse. She states:

If . . . we concentrated on documenting and theorizing the itinerary of the consolidation of Europe as sovereign subject, indeed sovereign and subject, then we would produce an alternative historical narrative of the "worlding" of what is today called "the Third World."

("The Rani of Sirmur," p. 247)

A worlding narrative of a colonized space operates to inscribe colonial discourse and hegemony on that space. This is a social construct because it is a "worlding of the world on uninscribed earth" ("The Rani of Sirmur," p. 253). A central way in which the practice of worlding occurs is through mapmaking, but there are ideological aspects as well. For instance, Spivak cites the example of an early-nineteenth-century British soldier traveling across India, surveying the land and people:

He is actually engaged in consolidating the self of Europe by obliging the native to cathect the space of the Other on his home ground. He is worlding *their own world*, which is far from mere uninscribed earth, anew, by obliging *them* to domesticate the alien as Master.

("The Rani of Sirmur," p. 253; emphases in original)

In effect, the colonized are made to experience their own land as belonging to the colonizer. Worlding and othering, then, are not simply carried out as matters of impersonal national policy, but are enacted by colonizers in local ways, such as the soldier traveling through the countryside.

Spivak often makes reference to the highly problematic nature of terms like "Third World," "Orient," and "Indian." For her, as for Said, these

terms are essentialist categories whose meanings hinge on binary oppositions that are of dubious usefulness because of their history and arbitrary
nature. Essentialist perspectives stress the idea that conceptual categories
name eternal, unchangeable characteristics or identities really existing in the
external world. Hence, a category like "Orient" becomes essentialist when
it is seen as naming a real place inhabited by people with the same characteristics and personality traits that are eternal and unchanging, and, by extension, inescapable because they are "naturally" possessed. Classic essentialist
categories include masculine/feminine and civilized/uncivilized. But essentialist categories are unstable because they are social constructions, not
universal names for "real" entities in the world. Further, the categories
Spivak discusses were constructed by a colonial discourse whose usage had
significant hegemonic and ideological implications and effects. A label like
"savage Indian" literally "others" its subject. That is, it forces the colonized
into a subaltern subject position not of their own choosing. Once located in
a particular subject position, the colonizing power can treat them accordingly, and the subjects often assume this role.

In her 1985 essay, "Subaltern Studies: Deconstructing Historiography,"
Spivak argues that although essentialism is highly problematic for the
knowledge it creates about an other, there is sometimes a political and social
need for what she calls **strategic essentialism**. By this she means a "*strategic
use of positivist essentialism in a scrupulously visible political interest*"
("Subaltern Studies: Deconstructing Historiography," p. 205). She argues
that it is necessary to assume an essentialist stand – for instance, speaking as
a woman or speaking as an Asian – so that the hegemony of patriarchal
colonial discourse can be disrupted and questioned. Spivak acknowledges
that the application of essentialist categories can have a salutary effect on
struggles against oppression and hegemonic power despite the problems
inherent in essentialist discourse: "I think it's absolutely on target to take a
stand against the discourses of essentialism . . . [b]ut *strategically* we
cannot" ("Criticism, Feminism, and the Institution," p. 11; emphasis in
original). Spivak is arguing that strategic essentialism is expedient, if only in
the short term, because it can aid in the process of revitalizing the sense of
personal and cultural worth and value of the dominated. One example of
this is when postcolonial cultures essentialize their pre-colonial past in order
to find a usable cultural identity.

The intersection of theory and social activism is a tension that runs
throughout Spivak's work. For instance, she has been critiqued for her view
of strategic essentialism on the grounds that she has given into the very
essentialist, universalist language to which she seems to be so adamantly
opposed. But for Spivak, the strategic use of essentialist categories is not a
matter of violating some notion of theoretical "purity," but rather is necessary from the perspective of social and political exigencies – and identity
politics – that require, among other things, certain kinds of discursive tools
in order to counter oppression and other ills. Spivak is also critical of

western feminists for sometimes ignoring the plight of women of color and, contrarily, for sometimes presuming to speak for non-western women on issues about which western feminists have no direct knowledge or experience. In this latter instance, speaking for non-western women is to once again mute the voices of women that western feminists are trying to assist. Such western feminist discourse creates non-western women as subaltern subjects and subverts their attempts to speak for themselves.

Although Spivak's concept of the subaltern is cited frequently in performance studies work that focuses on postcoloniality or disenfranchised identities, the field has not engaged with her ideas in depth. All of the ideas mentioned here could fruitfully be considered in relation to performance. Othering and worlding, for example, are performative practices that shape reality through their enactment. They are carried out through specific social, political, and military performances that could be examined in those terms. Similarly, some counter-hegemonic performances could be seen as attempts to counteract the impact of othering and worlding in specific contexts. Much the same is true for strategic essentialism, which quite literally entails a performance: the adoption of a specific identity role for a specific political and discursive purpose.

Although Spivak has never focused specifically on the connections between her ideas and performance studies, her writing suggests an awareness of those connections. In her criticism, Spivak discusses a broad range of texts, sometimes including performances alongside of literary works and films. Indeed, her own style of writing, which often interlaces critical and philosophical analyses with personal history and anecdote, and thus constitutes a performance of identity in itself, is a version of what is sometimes called "performative writing." I noted earlier that Spivak has used the metaphor of staging to describe the subject's relationship to the external discourses that influence her identity. In the same passage, Spivak extends that metaphor to describe the critic's social function: "One of the many tasks of the activist intellectual is to offer scrupulous and plausible accounts of the mechanics of staging" ("Acting Bits/Identity Talk," p. 781).

Further reading

By Spivak
"Acting Bits/Identity Talk." *Critical Inquiry* 18, no. 4 (1992): 770–803.
*"Can the Subaltern Speak?" In *The Post-Colonial Studies Reader*. Edited by Bill Ashcroft, Gareth Griffiths, and Helen Tiffin. London: Routledge, 1995.
A Critique of Postcolonial Reason: Toward a History of the Vanishing Present. Cambridge, MA: Harvard University Press, 1999.
In Other Worlds: Essays in Cultural Politics. New York: Methuen, 1987.
"Criticism, Feminism, and the Institution." In *The Post-Colonial Critic: Interviews, Strategies, Dialogues*. Edited by Sarah Harasym. New York: Routledge, 1990.
Outside in the Teaching Machine. London: Routledge, 1993.

*"The Rani of Sirmur: An Essay in Reading the Archives." *History and Theory* 24 (1985): 247–72.

The Spivak Reader: Selected Works of Gayatri Chakravorty Spivak. Edited by Donna Landry and Gerald MacLean. New York: Routledge, 1996.

"Subaltern Studies: Deconstructing Historiography." In *In Other Worlds: Essays in Cultural Politics*. New York: Methuen, 1987.

"Three Women's Texts and a Critique of Imperialism." *Critical Inquiry* 12 (1985): 243–61.

About Spivak

Merod, Jim. "Resistance to Theory: The Contradictions of Post-Cold War Criticism (with an Interlude on the Politics of Jazz)." In *Critical Theory and Performance*. Edited by Janelle Reinelt and Joseph Roach. Ann Arbor, MI: University of Michigan Press, 1992.

*Morton, Stephen. *Gayatri Chakravorty Spivak*. London: Routledge, 2002.

Morton, Stephen. *Gayatri Spivak (Key Contemporary Thinkers)*. Oxford: Blackwell, 2006.

Sanders, Mark. *Gayatri Chakravorty Spivak: Live Theory*. New York: Continuum, 2006.

Sharpe, Jenny. "The Violence of Light in the Land of Desire; Or, How William Jones Discovered India." *Boundary 2*, 20, no. 1 (1993): 26–46.

Young, Robert. "Spivak: Decolonization, Deconstruction." In *White Mythologies: Writing History and the West*. London: Routledge, 1990.

27 Hayden White

Key concepts

- fact as an event under description
- metahistory
- history as interpretation
- performativity
- tropology
- emplotment

Hayden White (1928–) was born in Tennessee and is an American intellectual and cultural historian associated with a narrativist view of history. He earned his BA from Wayne State University and his PhD from the University of Michigan in 1956. He held academic positions at the University of Rochester, University of California at Los Angeles, and Wesleyan University. In 1978, White became a professor in the History of Consciousness Program at the University of California at Santa Cruz. He was Presidential Professor of Historical Studies and is now University Professor Emeritus.

White approaches history from the perspective of language, suggesting that historical truth is always constructed through the narratives crafted by historians. Historical knowledge, therefore, is not simply the apprehension of an external reality, the truth of the past, but is a product of the historian's discourse. White's work typically takes aim at binary oppositions that pretend to organize "reality" in a logical, objective way. From White's perspective, for example, the traditional opposition of history's facts to literature's fictions is a false one. Congruent with this view, White's own work is located at the intersection of historiography and literary theory and has had a significant impact on both areas.

White acknowledges that his theoretical positions owe a great deal to both older historians and philosophers, as well as to contemporaries such as Northrop Frye and Kenneth Burke. He is critical of positivist views of history that assert that objective observation of the past can uncover historical truths. Such thinking is predicated on binary oppositions such as objectivity/subjectivity, truth/falsity, and fact/fiction. Instead, White argues that historians do not discover the facts "out there" but rather construct the "truths" of the historical past through narratives and tropes. Facts and truths are, therefore, primarily the domain of language embedded in partic-ular cultures. History, for White, is a discursive and rhetorical enterprise, not one of excavating objective, incontrovertible facts. White's ideas about historical discourse are contrary to traditional "realist" views of narrative which assume the posture of an omniscient narrator who tells a story char-acterized by uninterrupted flow. Such a narrative voice masks the usually fragmentary nature of historical sources and evidence. It creates the appear-ance of a complete and unambiguous story where none exists.

White describes a **"fact"** as **an event under description**. By this he means that historical factuality is constructed by historians in language. The fact cannot be separated from its verbal description. For White, historical events belong to the domain of reality, but facts belong to historical discourse. White does not deny the reality of past events, but he argues that any claims made about what "really" happened – the facts – are made in narratives of those events. The historian has no access to past reality, but only to discourses that assert facts about that past. In this sense, history is primarily a textual practice. When historians describe past events they are really talking about how other narratives have told the story of the past.

It is here that White makes one of his most important claims, namely that the past does not exist apart from historical representations of it, and those historical representations – historical texts – are themselves "literary arti-facts," that is, they too are part of history (see "Historical Text as Literary Artifact," in *Tropics of Discourse*). This claim is predicated, in part, on the observation that past events cannot be verified or "fact-checked." Differing interpretations of past events can be compared and criteria to determine the most compelling narrative can be determined, but the events themselves are inaccessible. On this basis, White claims that history must attend to lang-uage, in particular to historical narratives, traditions of history writing, the genres used to narrate a persuasive historical discourse, and other linguistic and textual aspects of telling history. In other words, history must also be **metahistory**. That is, it must be self-conscious and self-critical about the presumptions and strategies it employs in order to make sense of the past.

One of White's operating assumptions is that any mode of human inquiry, including historical research, has political or ideological implica-tions. In *The Content of the Form*, White notes:

> narrative is not merely a neutral discursive form that may or may not be used to represent real events in their aspect as developmental processes but rather entails ontological and epistemic choices with distinct ideo-logical and even specifically political implications.
>
> (*The Content of the Form*, p. ix)

Historical narratives and other representations of the past are ideological because they promote a perspective on the past that cannot be legitimized to "truth" or "objectivity" given the textual nature of the historiographical enterprise.

White's long career is punctuated by different phases of intellectual interest. Of this work, arguably the most influential is White's work on historical narrative as described in volumes such as *Metahistory: The Historical Imagination in Nineteenth-Century Europe* (1973), *Tropics of Discourse: Essays in Cultural Criticism* (1978), and *The Content of the Form: Narrative Discourse and Historical Representations* (1987). The first two volumes articulate White's arguments concerning historical narrative, discourse, and literary tropes. The latter text deals with issues of historical representation and narrative discourse.

In *Metahistory*, White uses structuralist ideas to understand the nature and function of historical discourses. It is in this volume that White makes his most important arguments about the narrative nature of history. White's narrativist philosophy of history sees the genre of literary narrative as central to the historian's craft. Against the Aristotelian distinction of fact from fiction that dominates contemporary historiography, White describes history as interpretation that takes the form of narrative. Here White draws a distinction between science as explanation and **history as interpretation**. Extending this distinction, White wants to expose history's scientific conceit, that is, history's traditional employment of explanatory models that are claimed to accurately describe facts and external events in a logical and objective manner. Against this conceit he presents history as historical narrative, a mode of discourse that sets forth interpretations of past events in a rhetorical manner. From this perspective, explanation does not present us with objective historical verities, but rather is best understood as a rhetorical device to persuade readers of the truth of a particular view of past events (cf. "emplotment" below). White, glossing Paul Ricoeur, uses J.L. Austin's concept of **performativity** to describe how historical narrative works: "a given emplotment of historical events is in the nature of a performative, rather than a constative, utterance" ("Historical Pluralism," p. 489). White thus suggests that historical narratives do not merely describe or report the objective facts, but actually create those "facts" through the act of recounting them. White's distinction between science and history can be charted as shown in the table.

White's theory of tropes (**tropology**) is central to arguments about historical writing he expresses in *Metahistory*. A trope is usually understood as a

Science	History
models	tropes
explanation	interpretation
logic	rhetoric

figure of speech, such as a metaphor. White, however, uses this term to refer to styles or modes of thought used by historical narratives to craft their discursive arguments. Through extensive research into the history of historiography, he shows how historical texts from particular periods have in common the use of certain tropes. For White, "troping is the soul of discourse" (*Tropics of Discourse*, p. 2), and it is one of the chief tasks of the historian to identify what tropes are used and to uncover their ideological ramifications.

Following Giambattista Vico and Kenneth Burke, White sets forth a hierarchical typology based on four master tropes: metaphor, metonymy, synecdoche, and irony. He understands the first three tropes as "naïve" tropes, "since they can only be deployed in the belief in language's capacity to grasp the nature of things in figurative terms" (*Metahistory*, pp. 36–37). Irony, on the other hand, is self-reflexive about the problem of universal truth claims, and is cognizant of the provisional nature of language. Thus White asserts:

> Irony . . . represents a stage of consciousness in which the problematical nature of language itself has become recognized. It points to the potential foolishness of all linguistic characterizations of reality as much as to the absurdity of the beliefs it parodies.
>
> (*Metahistory*, p. 37)

White also discusses modes of **emplotment** utilized by historical discourse. Just as with literary narratives, historical narratives have a plot structure that is utilized by the historian to tell the story of past events. Using Frye, White identifies four primary modes of emplotment: romance, comedy, tragedy, and satire. These modes of emplotment in turn are connected to modes of explanation and ideological implications based on the work of Stephen Pepper and Karl Mannheim. White understands these levels of interpretation in historical narrative as "structurally homologous with one another" (*Tropics of Discourse*, p. 70). He represents this homological relationship as shown in the table.

Mode of emplotment	Mode of explanation	Mode of ideological implication
romance	idiographic	anarchist
comedy	organicist	conservative
tragedy	mechanistic	radical
satire	contextualist	liberal

White makes it clear that his interpretive typologies are not meant as rigid containers into which all texts must clearly find a place:

> I do not suggest that these correlations necessarily appear in the work of a given historian; in fact, the tension at the heart of every historical masterpiece is created in part by a conflict between a given modality of

emplotment or explanation and the specific ideological commitment of its author.

(Tropics of Discourse, p. 70)

The narrative a historian creates from choices of plot, explanation, and ideology serves as an interpretation of past events. Historical interpretation has, according to White, at least three aspects: (1) the aesthetic (choice of narrative strategy); (2) the epistemological (choice of explanatory mode); and (3) the ethical (ideological choice). Historical discourse consists of these three interpretive aspects and thus presupposes a particular metahistory. "Every proper history presupposes a metahistory which is nothing but the web of commitments which the historian makes in the course of his interpretation on the aesthetic, cognitive, and ethical levels differentiated above" *(Tropics of Discourse*, p. 71). Thus, the issue for historians, according to White – and one that extends to the historian of performance – "is not, What are the facts? but rather, How are the facts to be described in order to sanction one mode of explaining them rather than another?" (*Tropics of Discourse*, p. 134).

White's theories on history as narrative present interesting possibilities for the study of theatre and performance. The questions he poses concerning the practice of history are as relevant to historical discourse on theatre and performance as they are to political or social history. Indeed, some theatre historians working "Towards a Postpositivist Theatre History" (Bruce McConachie, *Theatre Journal* 37, no. 4 (1985): 465–86) have turned to White and similar theorists for inspiration. White's theories also point toward the possibility of considering specific performances in terms of the ideas of narrative and its relationship to society he proposes. Performances are narratives, after all, in one sense or another, and the forms and tropes on which they rely are as socially imbricated as the practices of historians. White's metahistorical perspective encourages self-conscious reflection on these issues in all forms of communication. One could also argue that the dramaturgical turn in sociology and anthropology that has been a major influence on performance studies, in which human behavior is understood using ritual or dramatistic models (e.g. Victor Turner's concept of "social drama" or Erving Goffman's dramaturgical model for everyday behavior), narrativizes human behavior in ways that should be carefully scrutinized. Finally, it is possible to look to performance itself as a source for ways of telling stories and communicating information that challenge the typical narrative and tropic devices of written narratives.

Further reading

By White

The Content of the Form: Narrative Discourse and Historical Representations.
Baltimore, MD: Johns Hopkins University Press, 1987.

"Historical Pluralism." *Critical Inquiry* 12, no. 3 (1986): 480–93.

Metahistory: The Historical Imagination in Nineteenth-Century Europe. Baltimore, MD: Johns Hopkins University Press, 1973.

**Tropics of Discourse: Essays in Cultural Criticism.* Baltimore, MD: Johns Hopkins University Press, 1978.

About White

Bann, Stephen. "Analysing the Discourse of History." *Dalhousie Review* 64 (1984): 376–400.

Hutcheon, Linda. *A Poetics of Postmodernism: History, Theory, Fiction.* New York: Routledge, 1988.

Jenkins, Keith. "A Conversation with Hayden White." *Literature and History* 7 (1998): 68–82.

*Jenkins, Keith. *On "What is History?": From Carr and Elton to Rorty and White.* London: Routledge, 1995.

Konstan, David. "The Function of Narrative in Hayden White's *Metahistory*." *CLIO* 11, no. 1 (1981): 65–78.

LaCapra, Dominick. *Rethinking Intellectual History: Texts, Contexts, Language.* Ithaca, NY: Cornell University Press, 1983.

McCall, Michal M. and Becker, Howard S. "Performance Science." In *Performance: Critical Concepts*, Vol. III. Edited by Philip Auslander. London: Routledge, 2003. Originally published in *Social Problems* 37, no. 1 (1990): 117–32.

*Pihlainen, Kalle. "Of Closure and Convention: Surpassing Representation through Performance and the Referential." *Rethinking History* 6, no. 2 (2002): 179–200.

Turner, Victor. "Social Dramas and Stories about Them." In *Performance: Critical Concepts*, Vol. III. Edited by Philip Auslander. London: Routledge, 2003. Originally published in *Critical Inquiry* 7, no. 1 (1980): 141–68.

28 Raymond Williams

Key concepts

- Culture versus culture
- cultural studies
- ideal culture, documentary culture, social culture
- the structure of feeling
- dominant, residual, and emergent aspects of history

Raymond Williams (1921–88) was a British literary theorist, novelist, leading Marxist, and one of the founders of cultural studies. He was born in Wales and raised in a working-class family (his mother was a housewife, his father a railway signalman). In 1939 he entered Cambridge University on a scholarship. There he studied literature and was a member of the Cambridge University Socialist Club. His studies were interrupted in 1942 when he was called to military duty in World War II, serving as a tank commander. After the war, Williams returned to Cambridge to finish his degree.

After graduating from Cambridge, he worked in the Adult Education Department at Oxford University for fifteen years, during which time he wrote two major works, *Culture and Society, 1780–1950* (1958) and *The Long Revolution* (1961). He joined the faculty at Cambridge University as a lecturer in English and drama in 1961 and remained there for the rest of his career. Unlike most of the thinkers discussed in this volume, Williams took drama and theatre as his primary subjects for much of his career as both a scholar and a journalistic critic. Among his earliest books were *Drama from Ibsen to Eliot* (1952) and *Drama in Performance* (1954), in which he examines literary drama in relation to performance as a social practice in different historical eras. Significant works of the 1960s include *Modern Tragedy* (1966) and *Drama from Ibsen to Brecht* (1968). In 1975, he became Cambridge University's first Professor of Drama.

Williams approached literature from an interdisciplinary Marxist perspective. He explored ways in which social class hierarchy was expressed in literature, usually to the advantage of the upper classes. He was also interested in ways that modes of communication are connected to the material conditions of a society. His theories, especially those on culture, have impacted other intellectual currents such as New Historicism, and are often associated with Hayden WHITE's concept of metahistory and his focus on historiography as a form of interpretive narrative which is never disinterested with regard to matters of social power.

Williams's ideas about culture are foundational for the field now known as cultural studies. In *The Long Revolution*, his second major theoretical writing, he explores conceptual issues connected with the term culture. He distinguishes between **Culture** (capital C) and **culture** (lower-case c). Culture (capital C) is a moral and aesthetic term originally conceived by English writers such as the Victorian poet and humanist Matthew Arnold and the modern literary critic F.R. Leavis. In their discourse Culture means "high culture," that is, the sum total of civilization's greatest moral and aesthetic achievements. The not so hidden agenda of this idea of Culture, of course, is to assert and maintain social class – "high culture" and "high class" are synonymous. Against this view, Williams develops a concept of culture (lower-case c) in terms of the social. Here, culture is not comprised exclusively of those ideas and achievements deemed to be the high points of civilization. Rather, culture includes all products of human activity, including language, social, political, and religious ideas and institutions, and other expressions both conceptual and material. In other words, culture in this sense comprises all that humans create and enact in order to make sense of their existence.

It is this concept of culture that serves as the focal point for Williams's literary-cultural studies. By arguing that the concept of culture was irreducible to the products of an elite class, Williams helped create a new academic field – **cultural studies** (which Williams sometimes called "cultural science" to emphasize its connections to sociology) – that examines the everyday life of non-elite groups.

This conception of culture as social is for Williams one of "three general categories in the definition of culture" (*The Long Revolution*, p. 57): the ideal, the documentary, and the social. **Ideal culture** refers to the concept of culture as a "state or process of human perfection" measured by absolute or universal standards. In this instance, cultural analysis "is essentially the discovery and description, in lives and works, of those values which can be seen to compose a timeless order, or to have permanent reference to the universal human condition" (*The Long Revolution*, p. 57). **Documentary culture** approaches culture as a documentary record, a repository for the artifacts of cultural achievements, including literature, arts, and philosophy. Here, "culture is the body of intellectual and imaginative work, in which, in a detailed way, human thought and experience are variously recorded" (*The Long Revolution*, p. 57). Finally, **social culture**, as mentioned earlier, focuses on culture not simply in terms of the artifacts and achievements of high, elite culture, but also in terms of all the many ways that people conceive of and enact their lives. Thus culture encompasses the political, the religious, the economic, and popular culture, as well as all other modes of thought and practice by which people live in the world. For Williams, culture is not static, but rather is a process that on the one hand always asserts itself and acts on us, and on the other hand is constantly produced and changed by human beings. Cultural process flows both toward us and away from us. The idea of culture as social is meant to express this dynamism.

One of the by-products of Williams's egalitarian, non-elitist view of culture was that he laid a foundation for the study of popular culture. Because all human products and practices are considered valuable and available for cultural analysis, forms of what we now refer to as popular culture – such as television, film, pop/rock music, sports, and blogs – are as revealing about the nature of culture as high cultural productions. All cultural products count as culture. Williams studied popular culture explicitly in later works such as *Television: Technology and Cultural Form* (1974).

The three categories or definitions of culture are to be understood, says Williams, as a whole and in terms of the interactions and relationships pertaining between these three aspects of culture: "However difficult it may be in practice, we have to try to see the process as a whole, and to relate our particular studies . . . to the actual and complex organization" (*The Long Revolution*, p. 60). Williams therefore treated all dramatic representations, whether on stage, screen, radio, or television, as manifestations of the same set of cultural impulses, rather than cordoning them off as separate aesthetic and cultural forms. It is significant that his final analysis in *Drama in Performance*, a book that focuses on literary dramas and the conditions under which they were performed, is of a film. Williams saw theatre, drama, and all forms of culture as continuous with other practices characteristic of a given society. He argues in *Modern Tragedy*, for instance, that the strict literary meaning of the term tragedy should not be preferred to its informal meanings in everyday usage because all are expressive of how people understand their lives at specific times in specific places. Williams never relinquished the critic's interest in distinguishing good work from bad, but insisted that there was no correspondence between a work's quality and its cultural placement: "you can find kitsch in a national theatre and an intensely original play in a police series" ("Drama in a Dramatised Society," p. 305).

Several commentators, including Alan O'Connor and Shannon Jackson, have observed that one can trace the transition in Williams's thinking from a literary orientation to a cultural one through his work on drama and theatre: he moved from thinking primarily in textual terms to thinking of culture as something that is, like performance, enacted and embodied. By "looking both ways, at a stage and a text, and at a society active, enacted in them," Williams felt he was able to grasp "certain conventions which we group as society itself" ("Drama in a Dramatised Society," p. 311). In his examination of culture, Williams pays considerable attention to what he

calls **the structure of feeling,** a concept that originally emerged in his writing
on drama. According to Williams, a structure of feeling is the particular
character and quality of a shared cultural sense. Although the precise
meaning of this term changed over time in Williams's work, he used it
primarily to refer to the lived experience of a people – or a generation of
people – within particular cultural contexts. The lived experience includes
the interaction between "official" culture – laws, religious doctrine, and
other formal aspects of a culture – and the way that people live in their
cultural context. The structure of feeling is what imbues a people with a
specific "sense of life" and experience of community. It is comprised of the
set of particular cultural commonalities shared by a culture despite the individual differences within it. As Williams notes, the sense of commonality is
not necessarily shared throughout a culture, but is most likely the feeling of
the dominant social group. This cultural feeling is not typically expressed in
any verbal, rational mode of discourse, though it can often be located in
literary texts which reveal it only indirectly. Cultural analysis of the structure of feeling aims at uncovering how these shared feelings and values
operate to help people make sense of their lives and the different situations
in which the structure of feeling arises.

In *Marxism and Literature* (1977), Williams examines historiographical
issues, arguing that the cultural analyst must recognize the complex interactions that occur within historical contexts and be careful to avoid privileging
those dominant, empowered voices within it. In other words, rather than
view history as a progression of nameable cultural periods – in which each
period determines the one that follows – Williams wants to look at history
through the lens of cultural struggle and resistance. To this end, he posits
three terms "which recognize not only 'stages' and 'variations' but the
internal dynamic relations of any actual process" (*Marxism and Literature*,
p. 121). These are the "dominant," "residual," and "emergent" aspects of
historical periods.

The **dominant** aspects of a historical period are the systems of thought
and practice that dictate, or try to dictate, what can be thought and what
can be done – that is, the assertion of dominant values, morality, and meanings. For Williams, the concept of the dominant is related to the concept of
hegemony. The dominant is at once hegemonic, rigorously promoting the
interests of the empowered and suppressing the interests of others. But the
dominant does not stand uncontested. Williams reminds us that within any
cultural context, the "effective dominant culture" is always under siege by
alternative values, meanings, and practices that are not part of it. These
alternatives and oppositions to the dominant culture can be found in
"residual" and "emergent" forms.

The **residual** aspects of a historical period are past cultural formations.
These old values and meanings may have once been dominant but have now
been supplanted by the present dominant power. Aspects of these older
cultural forms may still be active in the present, exerting pressure on the

dominant forms, although they are generally subordinate to the dominant. In short, the residual can be both incorporated into the dominant culture, and at the same time can have aspects that stand in opposition or as an alternative to that culture.

The **emergent** aspects of a historical period are those newly emerging values, meanings, and practices that adumbrate future cultural directions and put pressure on the existing dominant culture. Cultural forms can never be frozen by the dominant culture. Dominant culture is always undergoing opposition by these new cultural forms that threaten to replace the dominant.

Williams views these three relations of cultural process as the ground where struggles over dominance and resistance to hegemony are waged. Further, this tripartite view of historical process requires us to view culture as dynamic rather than static, and to be mindful of the interactions and cross-fertilization of these three aspects of cultural movement and change. A statement about drama summarizes his view:

> The drama of any period, including our own, is an intricate set of practices of which some are incorporated – the known rhythms and movements of a residual but still active system – and some are exploratory – the difficult rhythms and movements of an emergent representation, rearrangement, new identification. Under real pressures these distinct kinds are often intricately and powerfully fused; it is rarely a simple case of the old drama and the new.
>
> ("Drama in a Dramatised Society," p. 308)

Williams's concepts of culture and history have much to offer theatre and performance studies, especially his view that cultural analysis means looking at any given cultural form or discourse in relation to others, not in isolation. Histories of theatre, for example, that fail to include Broadway musicals and other popular forms serve the interests of elitism without providing any sense of the complex ways in which different kinds of theatre are aligned with each other and with other forms of cultural expression at a given moment. His breaking down of the barriers between high and popular culture suggests a heterodox perspective, from which all aspects of the cultural picture need to be examined to understand the significance of any particular cultural element. Above all, Williams's perspective is a *materialist* perspective that emphasizes the importance of always looking at cultural discourses in relation to economic and social forces, not on the assumption that the economic and social determine the cultural, but with the understanding that they all interact to produce a structure of feeling that informs the way people experience their daily lives as much as their expressive culture.

Further reading

By Williams

Drama from Ibsen to Brecht. London: Chatto & Windus, 1968.

Drama from Ibsen to Eliot. London: Chatto & Windus, 1952.

*"Drama in a Dramatised Society." In *Performance: Critical Concepts*, Vol. II. Edited by Philip Auslander. London: Routledge, 2003. Originally published as a pamphlet by Cambridge University Press in 1975.

Drama in Performance. Maidenhead: Open University Press, 1991.

Keywords: A Vocabulary of Culture and Society, revised edn. New York: Oxford University Press, 1983.

* *The Long Revolution*, revised edn. New York: Columbia University Press, 1966.

* *Marxism and Literature*. New York: Oxford University Press, 1977.

Modern Tragedy. Stanford, CA: Stanford University Press, 1966.

The Raymond Williams Reader. Edited by John Higgins. Oxford: Blackwell, 2001.

Television: Technology and Cultural Form. London: Routledge, 2003.

About Williams

Eagleton, Terry (ed.). *Raymond Williams: Critical Perspectives*. Boston, MA: Northeastern University Press, 1989.

Eldridge, J.E.T. *Raymond Williams: Making Connections*. London: Routledge, 1994.

Higgins, John. *Raymond Williams: Literature, Marxism, and Cultural Materialism*. London: Routledge, 1999.

*Inglis, Fred. *Raymond Williams*. New York: Routledge, 1995.

Jackson, Shannon. "Why Modern Plays are Not Culture: Disciplinary Blind Spots." In *Performance: Critical Concepts*, Vol. II. Edited by Philip Auslander. London: Routledge, 2003. Originally published in *Modern Drama* 44, no. 1 (2001): 31–51.

*Kruger, Loren. "Placing the Occasion: Raymond Williams and Performing Culture." In *Views Beyond the Border Country: Raymond Williams and Cultural Politics*. Edited by Dennis L. Dworkin and Leslie G. Roman. New York: Routledge, 1993.

*McConachie, Bruce A. "Historicizing the Relations of Theatrical Production." In *Critical Theory and Performance*. Edited by Janelle Reinelt and Joseph Roach. Ann Arbor, MI: University of Michigan Press, 1992.

McGrath, John. "The Theory and Practice of Political Theatre." *Theatre Quarterly* 9 (1979): 43–54.

O'Connor, Alan. *Raymond Williams: Writing, Culture, Politics*. Oxford: Blackwell, 1989.

Prendergast, Christopher (ed.). *Cultural Materialism: On Raymond Williams*. Minneapolis, MN: University of Minnesota Press, 1995.

Thompson, John O. "Tragic Flow: Raymond Williams on Drama." *Screen Education* 34 (1980): 45–58.

29 Slavoj Žižek

Key concepts

* authentic act
* Buddhism
* over-identification

Slavoj Žižek (1949–) is a senior researcher in the Institute of Sociology at University of Ljubljana, Slovenia, his hometown. He has also been a visiting professor at several American and British universities.

Following formal education, Žižek was initially unable to acquire an academic post (purportedly because he was not sufficiently Marxist), and resorted to working as a translator. In the 1970s he helped form the Ljubljana Lacanians, a small band of young intellectuals interested in Jacques LACAN (Žižek himself spent time in Paris working with both Lacan and Jacques Alain-Miller, Lacan's mentee and son-in-law). The group took over the journal *Problemi*. Žižek's own contributions to this journal are often parodies or literary hoaxes. Once he wrote an anonymous negative review of one of his own books on Lacan. This kind of playfulness continues in more recent work.

Žižek is well known for his interpretations of popular culture, especially film and television (from Alfred Hitchcock's films to *The Matrix* to *The Oprah Winfrey Show*) in light of the theoretical canons of MARX, Lacan, and others. For this reason his work may appear to some as flippant and superficial. It is nothing of the sort. In all his work, Žižek seeks to develop a cultural theory that integrates psychoanalytic – especially Lacanian – conceptions of the subject with Marxian conceptions of ideology and polit-ical history. His description of his book series with Verso Press, *Wo es war* ("Where it was"), makes explicit the political wager involved in this intellec-tual venture: "the explosive combination of Lacanian psychoanalysis and Marxist tradition detonates a dynamic freedom that enables us to question the very presuppositions of the circuit of Capital" (*The Plague of Fantasies*, p. ii). Žižek draws on Lacanian psychoanalysis to conceive of a subject who can live and act within the order of things in ways that expose and subvert the logic of late capitalism – blow its circuits – thereby opening new possibilities for being in the world in relation to others.

Žižek is critical of Judith Butler's theory of subjectivity and social transformation which he believes cannot break free from the stronghold of the symbolic order. For him, the subversive, gender-troubling performances that she calls for "ultimately support what they intend to subvert, since the very field of such 'transgressions' is already taken into account" by the symbolic order, which he describes as a "gargantuan symbolic matrix embodied in a vast set of ideological institutions, rituals and practices." This order "is a much too deeply rooted and 'substantial' entity to be effectively undermined by the marginal gestures of performative displacement" described by Butler (*The Ticklish Subject*, p. 208).

Žižek returns to Lacan to develop a theory of political action in which the subject, unable to locate a universal common ground on which to stand outside the constraints of the symbolic order, nevertheless can act in such a way as to break the "hypnotic force" of that order. Such an **authentic act** is not simply one of several options within the order of things, but is in fact an act that exposes that order as a ruse and undermines its power over the subject, thus opening space for new kinds of social relations. In this way, Žižek insists on the possibility of a truly radical agency for subjects caught in the order of late capitalism, even while he acknowledges that such an agency cannot be solidly grounded. In a sense, the authentic act is a leap of faith, stepping off the false ground on which one stands without knowing exactly where one will land.

Some have seen psychoanalysis, including Lacanian psychoanalysis, as a basically conservative enterprise, in which the aim of analysis is to help the analysand reconcile herself to the symbolic order – to "work through" the in-breakings of the unconscious in such as way as to become happily integrated into the order of things, even if that order is in fact an illusion. To the contrary, Žižek insists that, for Lacan, psychoanalysis should enable the analysand to recognize that order as a "fake" and to break its hold on life (*The Fragile Absolute*, pp. 114–15). In this psychoanalytic conception of the symbolic order and the subject's relation to it, Žižek finds an approach to the Marxian problem of how to break loose from the circuits of capitalism.

Žižek finds one example of this radical potential – this opening toward the authentic act that can break the hypnotic force of the symbolic – in early **Buddhism** as expressed in the teachings of the Buddha.

> I can participate in this universal dimension [nirvana] *directly*, irrespective of my special place within the global social order. For that reason, Buddha's followers form a community of people who, in one way or another, have broken with the hierarchy of the social order and started to treat it as fundamentally *irrelevant*: In his choice of disciples, Buddha

pointedly ignored castes and (after some hesitation, true) even sexual difference.

> (*The Fragile Absolute*, p. 122; emphases in original)

Privileging social outcasts as exemplary, the community around the Buddha worked, stresses Žižek, to suspend established social hierarchy, thereby "unplugging" or "uncoupling" from its circuitry. Here, then, he recognizes a certain affinity with his own interest in concocting an "explosive combination" of Marxism and Lacanian psychoanalysis that "enables us to question the very presuppositions of the circuit of Capital."

Aside from a few pages on Bertolt Brecht, Žižek has written very little on theatre or performance and has had much more impact on cinema studies, an area in which he has worked, than on performance studies. Nevertheless, there are some themes in his work that might be of interest to those theorizing political performance. In his discussion of Brecht's early "learning plays," Žižek notes with approval that Brecht considered these plays as vehicles through which the performers would learn, not the audience:

> Brecht spoke about "bodily semiotics" . . . learning plays are to denounce and undermine the ruling ideology not on the level of its general theoretical propositions but on the level of the "microphysics of power," of patterns of behavior, of the rituals which materialize ideological propositions.
>
> (*Enjoy your Symptom*, p. 175)

The ideological underpinnings of those patterns would become clear to those who enacted them rather than those observing them from outside; this would enable the performers to understand the way ideology expresses itself even in their most mundane behavior and perhaps resist it. Žižek goes on to discuss Brecht's deemphasis of the heroic gesture and of "speaking truth to power" in favor of political tactics that are ultimately invisible because they bore from within rather than confront from without and make no truth-claims.

In other writings, Žižek has described the critical tactic of "excessive identification . . . : the enemy [of the ruling order] is the 'fanatic' who 'overidentifies' [with the dominant ideology] instead of keeping an adequate distance." Discussing the Slovenian activist group NSK, he states that the group "*'frustrates' the system (the ruling ideology) precisely insofar as it is not its ironic imitation, but over-identification with it* – by bringing to light the obscene superego underside of the system, **over-identification** suspends its efficiency" (as quoted by Inke Arns and Sylvia Sasse; emphasis in original). For Žižek, an effective tactic for critiquing the dominant system is not to stand apart from it but to take up a position that is uncomfortably close to it.

Further reading

By Žižek

Enjoy your Symptom! Jacques Lacan in Hollywood and Out. New York: Routledge, 2001.

The Fragile Absolute or, Why is the Christian Legacy Worth Fighting for? London: Verso, 2000.

On Belief. London: Routledge, 2001.

The Plague of Fantasies. London: Verso, 1997.

The Ticklish Subject: The Absent Centre of Political Ontology. London: Verso, 1999.

About Žižek

Arns, Inke and Sasse, Sylvia. "Subversive Affirmation: On Mimesis as a Strategy of Resistance." In *East Art Map: Contemporary Art and Eastern Europe.* Edited by IRWIN. London: Afterall, 2006.

*Burrill, Derek Alexander. "Out of the Box: Performance, Drama, and Interactive Software." *Modern Drama* 48, no. 3 (2005): 492–512.

Butler, Judith. "Arguing with the Real." In *Bodies that Matter: On the Discursive Limits of "Sex."* New York: Routledge, 1993.

Ichida, Yoshihiko. "Subject to Subject: Are we all Schmittians in Politics?" *borderlands e-journal* 4, no. 2 (2005). Online, available at: www.borderlandsejournal. adelaide.edu.au

Kubiak, Anthony. "As If: Blocking the Cartesian Stage." In *Psychoanalysis and Performance.* Edited by Patrick Campbell and Adrian Kear. London: Routledge, 2001.

Thomassen, Lasse. "The Politics of Lack." *Postmodern Culture* 11, no. 3 (2001): Online, available at: http://muse.jhu.edu/journals/postmodernculture